MARY

TEN TEST QUESTIONS FOR THE WORLD'S FINEST WOMAN

By William P. Welty, Ph.D.

Koinonia House

MARY: Ten Test Questions for the World's Finest Woman
A Protestant Theologian Studies the Life of Mary, the Mother of Jesus

 All Scripture quotations are from the *Holy Bible: International Standard Version®* (ISV®), v2.0. Copyright © 1996-2016 by The ISV Foundation. All rights reserved internationally. Used by permission. Visit the ISV Foundation at http://isv.org.

A summary outline of this work was published previously in a public lecture series presented at the Single Parents Fellowship of the Evangelical Free Church of Fullerton, California. A small portion of this work was originally developed for and released by the ISV Foundation. Our thanks to the late George Burch, whose instruction in the Gospel narratives inspired me to deeper studies about the life of Mary and to the production of this detailed analysis.

Appendix One contains material researched and written by Timothy Dunkin. Copyright © 2016 by Timothy Dunkin. Used by permission. Appendix Two contains material compiled and written by Dr. Chuck Missler from his commentary on *2 John*. Copyright © 2009 by Koinonia House. Used by permission.

On the Cover: Portrait of Mary, the mother of Jesus extrapolated from the Shroud of Turin painted and Copyright © 2016 by Dean Packwood. All rights reserved internationally. Used by permission of the artist. Please visit http://packwood.deviantart.com/ or https://www.youtube.com/DLPackwood for more information.

© Copyright 2016 William P. Welty Ph.D.
Published by Koinonia House
P.O. Box D
Coeur d'Alene, ID 83816-0347
www.khouse.org

ISBN: 978-1-57821-662-8

PRINTED IN THE UNITED STATES OF AMERICA

In Remembrance of
ROBERT F. "BOBBY" D'AUSILIO
17 November 1933 – 15 March 2016

Arguably considered by those who knew him to be the foremost authority on American aerospace industry of the twentieth century, Bobby was a founding member of and senior aerospace technology advisor to the author's *Super-Wide Area Network Satellite (SWANsat)* project. He passed away from natural causes on 15 March 2016.

In the 1960s and 1970s, Bobby served as the *Apollo Program Communications Payload Manager.* He has been credited with developing the dramatic rescue plan that successfully retrieved the Apollo 13 crew from orbit, and thus saving the lives of the three crew members on board, following a catastrophic failure of the spacecraft. It was my privilege to contact him every 3rd week of July since we met in January 1992 to congratulate him personally on the anniversary of the Apollo 11 moon landing.

One of the key developers of the world-renowned *Geo-Positioning Satellite System,* Bobby taught me how to aim for excellence while doing all things to the glory of God.

He passed away while we were in New Zealand readying for publication our latest theological treatise on the life of Mary, the mother of Jesus of Nazareth.

Along with his wife Sylvia, Bobby was a practicing Catholic. He held this Protestant theologian in very high regard. He is very deeply missed. Rest in peace, my friend. May God reward you at the End of Days.

DEDICATION

TO DR. MARGIT BRANDL
(http://brokenmuses.com)

My elegant, sophisticated, European telecommunications attorney friend and world class modern art photographer. May you soon meet and become acquainted, both in this life and also in the one to come, with the magnificent Son of the amazing woman described so inadequately in this work.

TO KRISTIN QUINN
(http://kristinquinn.com)

My kind, thoughtful, loving, and drop-dead gorgeous world-class fashion model friend. A New York-based actress/entrepreneur, her character, courage, and life activities remain a perennial source of encouragement to me.

TO CHARLES ROY WELTY
(http://charleswelty.net and http://weltybrothersstudios.com)

My twin brother, whose phenomenal talent at motion picture and radio scriptwriting is a source of continual amazement to me. May God strengthen you to complete the tasks to which he has called you in the days and years ahead.

Thanks to *Timothy Dunkin* for permission to reprint his essay in Appendix One: Does Isaiah 7:14 Prophesy that a *Virgin* Would Conceive? and to *Koinonia Institute Chairman and Founder Dr. Chuck Missler* for permission to utilize material from his commentary on 2 John in Appendix Two.

Thanks also to *Dean Packwood*, for extending permission to utilize his forensic portrait of Mary, the mother of Jesus, extrapolated from the *Shroud of Turin*.

And thanks to the *Rev. Msgr. Charles Mangan*, Director of the Marian Apostolate for the Diocese of Sioux Falls, South Dakota, and the Vicar for Consecrated Life and the Canonical Adviser to the Most Reverend Paul J. Swain, D.D., the Bishop of Sioux Falls, for agreeing to review this work from a Roman Catholic perspective. No endorsement by Father Mangan or by the Roman Catholic Church is implied by our acknowledgment.

Special thanks are due to *Jeanne O'Neill* and *Ron Kessler*
for their generous hospitality provided to me during the writing
of this book, and to Jeanne's parents *Rosemarie* and *Frank*,
whose company helped provide a welcome break for a few days
from Jeanne's and Ron's barking dogs…all six of them,
not counting the two that belong to Jeanne's daughter *Pam*.
And from the cats. I do remember the cats…

Lastly, a special mention is due to *Miss Alexa*, the finest five year
old young lady any theologian would ever want to meet.

Table of Contents

Table of Figures

An Introduction to the World's Finest Woman

Maybe It's Time You Learned the Truth...

The community of faith worldwide knows her as the finest woman who ever lived. Born in obscurity to a distant descendant of Israel's magnificent King David, Christians believe that Mary, the mother of Jesus of Nazareth, was honored by the Creator of the Universe to be the person through whom God himself would visit His own Creation, reconciling his people to himself.

No matter what you may have thought you knew before about this first century paragon of virtue and faith, there's a good possibility that you've been misinformed about her.

In fact, chances are you've been wrong from the start about the most remarkable woman who ever walked the dusty roads of first century Israel during the height of the Roman Empire's domination over the Middle East.

Mary Isn't Who You Think She Is

More than twenty centuries have come and gone since a teenaged virgin became the mother of God's incarnate Son. As a result, far too much myth has grown up around the person and story surrounding the woman who became one of the foundational figures of human history. What the New Testament records themselves tell us about the life of Mary, the mother of Jesus, is fascinating enough in its own right that we can learn a lot from studying what the New Testament says about her without getting embroiled in two thousand years of extraneous ecclesiastical convention.

In this work, we will attempt to pull back the dusty curtain of historically inaccurate tradition in order to introduce you to the very human, but utterly magnificent character of Mary, the mother of the Messiah, as she struggles to pass *Ten Test Questions for the World's Finest Woman* that are presented to her in the passages recorded in the New Testament that mention her. Each of these ten spiritual challenges provide a fresh new opportunity to refine her faith and trust in God.

As we'll see in our study, Mary the mother of Jesus of Nazareth passed nine out of the ten tests splendidly. She stumbled in her faith only once, but ultimately prevailed, obtaining an astonishing 95% on her series of spiritual tests of her faith and obedience to God's plans and purposes for her life.

In our analysis that follows of every passage recorded in the New Testament in which Mary is referred to or mentioned by name, you'll learn why the mother of the world's most famous rabbi from Nazareth rose from literal obscurity to become one of the greatest pivotal figures in all of human history, treasured by millions of people throughout the centuries, and fulfilling Mary's prophecy recorded in Luke 1:48 that "from now on, all generations will call me blessed."

ISLAMIC RESPECT FOR MARY

Islam, which takes a position of *animosity* toward Christianity with respect to its doctrine of the Incarnation, pays respectful homage to the mother of Jesus, calling her *Maryām* (Arabic: مريم), mentioning her more often in the Qur'an than does the entire New Testament! It

Figure 1: The Ka'aba in Mecca.
Image source: https://upload.wikimedia.org/-
ia/commons/f/f3/Kaaba_mirror_edit_jj.jpg

distinguishes her within Islamic history by making her the only woman mentioned by name in the Qur'an. According to the Qur'an, Mary's son Jesus (known in Islam as *Isa*) was born miraculously by the will of God, without a natural father. She is described in the Qur'an as a morally pure and virtuous woman, and is unmistakably described as having been a virgin at the time of Jesus' conception.

It further describes her as having been chosen "above the women of all nations" (*Sura 3 [Al Imran], ayah 42*). Of the 114 *suras* (chapters) that comprise the Qur'an, only eight of them are named after individuals, and Mary is one of them, being referred to as an example for other believers to emulate. The Qur'an's *Makkan sura 19* (Arabic: سورة مريم), consisting of 98 *ayat* (verses) and named *Mary*, after her, mentions her in verses 16-34. So popular is she in certain denominations of Islam that Qur'anic quotations relating to Mary may often be observed inscribed within the

Figure 2: Mary and Jesus in Persian miniature.
Image source: https://upload.-
wikimedia.org/wiki-pedia/
commons/f/f4/Virgin_Mary_
and_Jesus_¬%28old_Persian_-
miniature%29.jpg

mihrab [1] of various mosques throughout the world, including the *Hagia Sophia*, located in Istanbul, Turkey.[2]

MARY AND JESUS IN THE TALMUD

The Jewish *Talmud* isn't so friendly with respect to its treatment of Mary, the mother of Jesus. While there are almost as many scholarly opinions as to what the *Talmud* may or may not be saying about Mary, the extremely complex set of traditions that inform the compilation of this Hebrew and Aramaic language commentary on the Torah has resulted in wide divergence of opinion regarding what this document has to say about both Jesus and his mother Mary. Much of the debate about which passages refer to Mary and Jesus stems from an

Figure 3: The Babylonian Talmud. Image source: https://upload.wikimedia.org/ wikipedia/commons/3/38/-Talmud_set.JPG

unfortunate history of persecution of the Jewish community by the Christian community and subsequent attempts by Talmudic scholars to redact the *Talmud* in order to minimize the risks attendant to Jewish adherents possessing a book that could be interpreted by Christians as containing blasphemous comments about Mary and her son. In the *Talmud*, Jesus is claimed to have been fathered by Mary's Roman soldier lover, who is named in that book as *Pandera*. (Some editions read *Panthera*.) Greek scholars recognize the name as a Latinized rendition and corruption of the Greek term παρθένος (*parthénos*), which means "virgin." Writing c. 170 AD, the Platonic philosopher Celsus observed that Jesus:

> *...came from a Jewish village and from a poor country woman who earned her living by spinning. He says that she was driven*

---

1   I.e., a semicircular niche carved into the wall of a mosque, intended to indicate the *qibla*, which is the direction toward the *Ka'aba* in Mecca, which Muslims are to face when praying.

2   For further reading, see https://en.wikipedia.org/wiki/Mary_in_Islam.

out by her husband, who was a carpenter by trade, as she was convicted of adultery. Then he says that after she had been driven out by her husband and while she was wandering about in a disgraceful way she secretly gave birth to Jesus. He states that because he [Jesus] was poor he hired himself out as a workman in Egypt, and there tried his hand at certain magical powers on which the Egyptians pride themselves; he returned full of conceit, because of these powers, and on account of them gave himself the title of God . . . the mother of Jesus is described as having been turned out by the carpenter who was betrothed to her, as she had been convicted of adultery and had a child by a certain soldier named Panthera.[3]

The Babylonian *Talmud* clearly refers to an anonymous person who is alleged to have brought witchcraft from Egypt, calling him only "the son of Pandera," and further alleging that his mother Mary committed adultery.[4] Also:

- The Babylonian *Shabbat 104b* asks "Was he the son of Stara (and not) the son of Pandera?" (Editions or MSS: Oxford 23, Soncino); and,

- The Babylonian *Sanhedrin 67a* asks "Was he the son of Stara (and not) the son of Pandera?" (Editions or MSS: Herzog 1, Karlsruhe 2); and,

- The Babylonian *Shabbat 104b* refers to her "husband Stada, lover Pandera" (Editions or MSS: Vatican 108, Munich 95, Vilna); and,

- The Babylonian *Sanhedrin 67a* refers to her "husband Stara, lover Pandera" (Editions or MSS: Herzog 1, Barco); and,

- The Babylonian *Shabbat 104b* refers to her "husband Pappos, mother Stada" (Editions or MSS: Vilna, Munich 95); and,

---

3   Cited by Peter Schäfer, *Jesus in the Talmud*, Princeton University Press, 2007. p 18-19. See also Bernhard Pick, *The Talmud: What It Is and What It Knows of Jesus and His Followers*, 1887 (Kessinger Publishing, LLC, 2007. p 117-120),
4   Peter Schäferr, pp 15–24, 133–141.

- The Babylonian *Sanhedrin 67a* refers to her "husband Pappos, mother Stada" (Editions or MSS: Vilna, Munich 95); and,

- The Babylonian *Shabbat 104b* refers to Jesus' "mother Miriam who let grow (her) women's hair" (Editions or MSS: Vilna, Oxford 23, Soncino); and,

- The Babylonian *Sanhedrin 67a* refers to "his mother Miriam who let grow (her) women's hair" (Editions or MSS: Karlsruhe 2, Munich 95).

THE MOTHER OF JESUS: A POINT OF CONTENTION FOR CATHOLICS AND PROTESTANTS

The Protestant Christian community has a tendency to give Roman Catholics a whole lot of grief concerning that Church's views about Mary, the mother of Jesus the Messiah. But then again, the animosity is all-to-often reciprocated in kind by the Catholics to the Protestants. If the truth were to be faced honestly by the Protestant side of the historically internecine dispute between the two opposite sides of the Christian Church, I suspect that most Protestants today don't have a clue as to what's really behind the significant differences between what Protestants believe and what Catholic dogma teaches. For example, how many Protestants do you know who can even begin to articulate what the function of the *Magisterium* is?[5] The same can be said about many Roman Catholic believers. For example,

Figure 4: Portrait of John Calvin (10 July 1509 – 27 May 1564) by Hans Holbein the Younger. Image source: https://upload. wikimedia.org/wikipedia/commons/c/ c5/John_Calvin_by_Holbein.png

---

5   The *Magisterium* is the authority to proscribe what are considered to be the authentic teachings of the Roman Catholic Church as such authority is vested in the Pope as Bishop of Rome and the bishops who attend to him. The teachings of Scripture and of Church tradition are considered by Catholic dogma to constitute together as a single repository of the Word of God, as entrusted to the Church. For further study, see https://en.wikipedia.org/wiki/Magisterium.

when is the last time you've known a Catholic who has taken the time to read the tenets of the *Council of Trent?* That was the Catholic Church's official response to the Reformation. It originally was convened by Pope Paul III, and met for 25 sessions between 13 December 1545 and 4 December 1563 in Trent, Italy. Sessions 9-11 were held in Bologna, Italy in

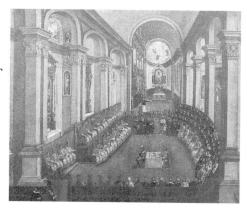

Figure 5: Council of Trent, meeting in the Santa Maria Maggiore, Trent, Italy. Image source: https://upload.wikimedia.org/ wikipedia/-commons/c/ca/Council_of_Trent.JPG

1547. Now as far as Protestant theology goes, do you know *any* Protestants or Catholics who've even *started* to read John Calvins's *Institutes of the Christian Religion* or the *Westminster Confession?*

DIFFERING TRADITIONS: THE PROTESTANT/CATHOLIC DIVIDE

Protestant Christians prefer to derive their teachings concerning Mary, the mother of Jesus of Nazareth, directly from the Biblical narratives alone, not relying on extra-canonical works or historical traditions. Roman Catholic theology honors Scriptural tradition, but also relies on a number of supplemental statements handed down over the centuries in order to systematize its views about her and about her life.

Among these supplemental dogmas that the Roman Catholic Church teaches, but which Protestantism rejects, are the doctrines of *The Immaculate Conception* and *The Assumption of Mary.*

The former doctrine states that the conception of Mary took place without transmitting to her the fallen, sinful nature of humanity through the womb of her mother (who is named in Catholic tradition as *Saint Anne,* but who remains anonymous in the New Testament). The Catholic Church holds the view that Mary was conceived by normal biological means, as do the Protestants. However,

Figure 6: De hemelvaart van Maria by Reubens, c. 1626.
Image source: https://upload.wikimedia. org/wikipedia/commons/e/ed/Baroque_ Rubens_Assumption-of-Virgin-3.jpg

Catholic dogma also teaches that God acted supernaturally to keep Mary free from sin (i.e., to keep her *immaculate*) at her conception.[6]

The dogma of the Immaculate Conception was not defined precisely until 8 December 1854, when Pope Pius IX did so via his papal bull *Ineffabilis Deus.*[7]

The Roman Catholic doctrine called the *Assumption of Mary* is a logical follow-on to the Immaculate Conception. It was dogmatically declared on 1 November 1950 via an apostolic constitution called *Munificentissimus Deus.*[8] It states that Mary was bodily taken up into heaven at the end of her earthly life, following the pattern described in the Old Testament concerning Elijah the prophet and Enoch. There is no biblical support for this teaching. It came to be promulgated because human death springs from human beings having a sinful nature, and therefore Mary could not have died if she had been born without possessing such a nature.

THE DEMURE TEENAGER FROM NAZARETH

The text of the New Testament Gospel narratives does not tell us much about the personal background of Mary, the mother of Jesus. We do know quite a bit about the genealogy of Jesus from

---

6 This doctrine is commonly misidentified with the Christian view of the *virgin conception* of Jesus, which the New Testament claims occurred without the participation of a human father.

7 For further reading, see https://en.wikipedia.org/wiki/Ineffabilis_Deus.

8 For further reading, see https://en.wikipedia.org/wiki/Munificentissimus_Deus.

two versions of it that have been set forth for us in the books written by Matthew and Luke, respectively. Both versions differ slightly from each other. Matthew's edition traces the lineage of Mary and her son, starting with Abraham and proceeding forward in time down through history, ending with Mary's husband Joseph. You can read all about it in Matthew 1:2-16:

Figure 7: Edward Frampton's The Annunciation. Image source: http://jesus-story.net/ images/annuncia33.jpg

²Abraham fathered Isaac, Isaac fathered Jacob, and Jacob fathered Judah and his brothers. ³Judah fathered Perez and Zerah by Tamar, Perez fathered Hezron, Hezron fathered Aram, ⁴Aram fathered Amminadab, Amminadab fathered Nahshon, and Nahshon fathered Salmon. ⁵Salmon fathered Boaz by Rahab, Boaz fathered Obed by Ruth, Obed fathered Jesse, ⁶and Jesse fathered King David. David fathered Solomon by the wife of Uriah, ⁷Solomon fathered Rehoboam, Rehoboam fathered Abijah, Abijah fathered Asaph, ⁸Asaph fathered Jehoshaphat, Jehoshaphat fathered Joram, Joram fathered Uzziah, ⁹Uzziah fathered Jotham, Jotham fathered Ahaz, Ahaz fathered Hezekiah, ¹⁰Hezekiah fathered Manasseh, Manasseh fathered Amos, and Amos fathered Josiah. ¹¹Josiah fathered Jechoniah and his brothers at the time of the deportation to Babylon.

Figure 8: Virgin of the Veil by Ambrogio Borgognone, 1500. Image source: http://jesus-story. net/images/Borgognone_Virgin_- and_Child.jpg

¹²After the deportation to Babylon, Jechoniah fathered Salathiel, Salathiel fathered Zerubbabel, ¹³Zerubbabel fathered Abiud, Abiud fathered Eliakim, Eliakim fathered Azor, ¹⁴Azor fathered Zadok, Zadok fathered Achim, Achim fathered Eliud, ¹⁵Eliud fathered Eleazar, Eleazar fathered Matthan, and Matthan fathered Jacob. ¹⁶Jacob fathered Joseph, the husband of Mary, who was the mother of Jesus, who is called the Messiah.

Matthew's rendition presents the genealogy of Jesus through Mary's *husband* Joseph (see verse 16, above) who served as "foster father," so to speak, of Jesus. Matthew tells us that Mary's husband Joseph was a descendant of David through King Solomon's son Solomon,[9] while Luke's Gospel traces the lineage of Jesus backward in time through another of David's sons, Nathan (see Luke 3:31, below), down throughout history and ending with Adam, the first man. You can read it in Luke 3:23-38:

²³Jesus himself was about 30 years old when he began his ministry. He was (as legally calculated) the son of Joseph, the son of Heli, ²⁴the son of Matthat, the son of Levi, the son of Melchi, the son of Jannai, the son of Joseph, ²⁵the son of Mattathias, the son of Amos, the son of Nahum, the son of Esli, the son of Naggai, ²⁶the son of Maath, the son of Mattathias, the son of Semein, the son of Josech, the son of Joda, ²⁷the son of Joanan, the son of Rhesa, the son of Zerubbabel, the son of Shealtiel, the son of Neri, ²⁸the son of Melchi, the son of Addi, the son of Cosam, the son of Elmadam, the son of Er, ²⁹the son of Joshua, the son of Eliezer, the son of Jorim, the son of Matthat, the son of Levi, ³⁰the son of Simeon, the son of Judah, the son of Joseph, the son of Jonam, the son of Eliakim, ³¹the son of Melea, the son of Menna, the son of Mattatha, the son of Nathan, the son of David, ³²the son of Jesse,

---

9   See Matthew 1:16, which tells us that "Jacob fathered Joseph, the husband of Mary, who was the mother of Jesus, who is called the Messiah."

*the son of Obed, the son of Boaz, the son of Salmon, the son
of Nahshon, ³³the son of Amminadab, the son of Admin,
the son of Arni, the son of Hezron, the son of Perez, the son
of Judah, ³⁴the son of Jacob, the son of Isaac, the son
of Abraham, the son of Terah, the son of Nahor, ³⁵the son
of Serug, the son of Reu, the son of Peleg, the son of Eber,
the son of Shelah, ³⁶the son of Cainan, the son of Arphaxad,
the son of Shem, the son of Noah, the son of Lamech, ³⁷the son
of Methuselah, the son of Enoch, the son of Jared, the son
of Mahalaleel, the son of Cainan, ³⁸the son of Enos, the son
of Seth, the son of Adam, the son of God.*

Do note, if you would, how Luke's edition of the genealogy presents Jesus as being a literal descendant of David through David's younger son Nathan (see Luke 3:31) as it traces Jesus' lineage to Mary, whose own father bore the same name Joseph as did her future husband.¹⁰ Also please note how Luke describes Joseph as being "legally calculated" as being Jesus' foster father. That's because Joseph *raised Jesus* as his own legally adopted son without having been his biological father. To employ more modern terminology as a description of his relationship to Jesus, today we would call Joseph the foster father of Jesus, and *not* his birth father.

While debate has raged for generations about the so-called "discrepancy" that appears to exist between the two separate genealogical listings, the reason for the alleged discrepancy is really quite simple: the two genealogies were recorded to document why *Jesus could never have been a direct biological son of Joseph*, Mary's betrothed husband. If Jesus had been Joseph's literal son, he would have been a descendant of David through King Solomon and therefore he would have been *ineligible* to sit on the throne of David. That's because during the lifetime of the prophet Jeremiah, God cursed the genealogical line of David's son Solomon by declaring in Jeremiah 22:30 about Solomon's descendants who would be born after Jechoiachin:

---

10 See Luke 3:23, which tells us that "Jesus himself was about 30 years old when he began his ministry. He was (as legally calculated) the son of Joseph..."

> ³⁰ *This is what the* LORD *says:*
> *'Write this man off as childless,*
>   *a man who does not prosper in his lifetime.*
> *None of his descendants will succeed*
>   *in sitting on the throne of David,*
>   *or ever ruling in Judah again.*

In contrast to the above, Luke's Gospel records that Jesus himself descended from David through David's younger son Nathan, who was probably named by David in tribute to David's lifelong friend, the prophet Nathan. Scripture says *nothing* about any divine curse on the lineage of David through David's younger son Nathan. Therefore, as the biological son of Mary only, Jesus was *biologically and legally qualified* to sit on the throne of Israel as the lawful descendant of King David.

A MODERN FORENSICS IMAGE OF MARY?

Nobody knows what she looked like. One of the prophetic descriptions of the Messiah contained in the writings of the Old Testament prophet Isaiah mention him as being of no particular attractiveness. Isaiah 53:2b describes the Messiah like this:

> *…he had no form and he had no majesty*
>   *that we should look at him,*
> *and there is no attractiveness*
>   *that we should desire him.*

No renderings of her likeness appear to have been made by the early believers in great Mary's greater Son.

Dean Packwood produced a rendering of what Mary might have looked like by referencing an image that appears to have been imprinted on the Shroud of Turin.[11] He painted what has been described as a pseudo-forensic image. (See figure 10, on page 13.)

The New Testament makes it clear that Jesus was the biological descendant of Mary *only*. Joseph made no biological contribution

---

11 See http://packwood.deviantart.com/art/Mary-Mother-of-Jesus-Painting-600089030
   or https://youtu.be/bm5oAgxJduI

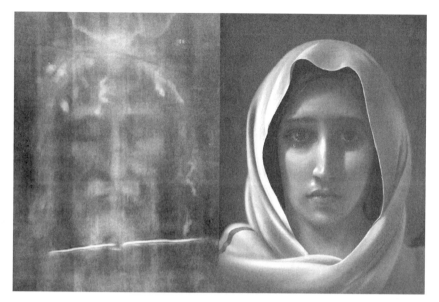

Figure 9: Shroud of Turin photographic negative image of the face of a crucified man some believe to have been imprinted on the burial shroud of Jesus of Nazareth. Image source: https://en.wikipedia. org/~wiki/Shroud_of_Turin

Figure 10: Modern forensic projection of image of Mary, the Mother of Jesus painted by Dean Packwood from referencing the Shroud of Turin. Image source: http://packwood. deviantart.com/art/Mary-Mother-of-Jesus-Painting-600089030

to his genetic structure. Accordingly, since the source code for Jesus' DNA would have come only from Mary, Jesus of Nazareth would have displayed an appearance containing the masculine equivalence or parity of Mary's physical features. For example, her eye color would have been inherited by Jesus in his incarnation, as would her hair color and skin color.

However, given Isaiah's prophetic indication quoted above that the Messiah would bear no outward attractiveness to the eye, we believe that the tendency of post-first century artists to portray her as demurely beautiful may well be inaccurate. Instead, she could have been a rather plain looking young lady, and perhaps a bit average in outward appearance.

BACKGROUND TO THE NEW TESTAMENT RECORDS REGARDING MARY

THE GOSPEL OF MATTHEW

The ***Gospel of Matthew*** mentions Mary by name six times in Matthew 1:16, 18, 20; 2:11; and 13:55. Note that five of these six instances are within the context of the infancy narrative of Jesus. Matthew's record of the life of Jesus is widely perceived as having been written to a largely Jewish audience, since it focuses on what Jesus had to say, presenting him as the rightful Messiah entitled to sit on David's throne.

Early Christian tradition identified the four Gospels with icons based on the four faces of angelic creatures described in the books of Ezekiel and Revelation (cf. Ezekiel 1:10; 10:14; Rev. 4:7ff; 21:13ff) and also reflecting the encampment of ancient Israel in the wilderness. Matthew's Gospel has been symbolized as a lion, representing the camp of Judah standing east of the Tabernacle that serves as an expression of the character of the Messiah's royalty by presenting Jesus as King of kings and Lord of lords.

The book is traditionally attributed to Matthew, a descendent of Levi who also served for a time as a tax collector for local Roman authorities. In that capacity, Matthew would have been skilled in the art of *tachygraphy*, an ancient Greco-Roman system of shorthand that could have enabled him to record the public discourses of Jesus in substantially a word-for-word format.

Many conservative scholars date this work to sometime after the destruction of the Jerusalem Temple in 70 AD, even though evidence exists that this work—along with the rest of the New Testament—was actually completed antecedent to that date. Once school of textual criticism suggests that Matthew was the first writer to have composed his Gospel, originally re-coding its contents in Hebrew or Aramaic, with copies of it translated or transcribed at a later time into Greek for dissemination to the larger Christian community. The Messianic Theme of this work is *The Gospel for Jews—What did the Messiah Say?*

The Gospel of Mark

The **Gospel of Mark** mentions Mary by name only once (Mark 6:3), but refers to her without mentioning her name twice in Mark 3:31-32. Mark's record of the life of Jesus is widely perceived as having been written to a largely Roman audience. Accordingly, this work focuses on what Jesus did as it presents him as a forceful man of action in control of the events surrounding him as he served those in need while demonstrating the great power and ability of Jesus as the Messiah, the Son of God.

Many see this work as being written to provide courage and confidence to believers who were being persecuted in the mid-'60s AD. Mark records fewer parables than does Matthew and Luke, but describes more miracles in which the hand of Jesus is frequently mentioned to emphasize a sense of his personal service. Portions of the final addendum are disputed as to authenticity by some scholars due to conflicting evidence relating to the textual transmission history of parts of the record of post-resurrection events leading up to the ascension of Jesus to heaven.

Mark's Gospel has been symbolized as an ox, representing the camp of Ephraim standing west of the Tabernacle and serving as an expression of the character of the Messiah's labor and service by presenting Jesus as the servant of God and the servant of men.

Some scholars hold that this work was the first written Gospel rather than the Gospel of Matthew. Traditionally attributed to John Mark, a companion of Peter and Paul in several missionary activities, it is generally agreed that the Gospel of Mark was written in Rome, first intended for use by Roman citizens living there. Pertinent evidence for this theory includes frequent quotation of Aramaic words, followed by a translation of them, along with explanations of Jewish customs clearly intended primarily for non-Jewish readers.

Conservative scholars who hold to a very early date for the writing of this Gospel attribute this work to the late '60s or early '70s AD, most likely before the destruction of the Jerusalem Temple in 70 AD. Some note that allusions to persecution contained in the work (cf. 8:34-38; 10:38-40) seem to be too general to have been written down after the commencement of persecution under Nero in ca. 60 AD. Therefore it is surmised that a more likely post-persecution date for the writing of this work would have resulted in a more intense literary focus consistent with such persecution, had this book been composed at a date later than before 64 AD.

The Messianic Theme of this work is *The Gospel for Romans— What did the Messiah Do?*

THE GOSPEL OF LUKE

The ***Gospel of Luke*** mentions Mary by name twelve times in Luke 1:27, 30, 34, 38, 39, 41, 46, 56; 2:5, 16, 19, and 34. All of these instances are within the context of the infancy narrative of Jesus. Luke's record of the life of Jesus is widely perceived as having been written to a largely Greek audience, or at least to gentiles in general. Accordingly, this work focuses on who Jesus knew as it presents him in close interaction with men, women, and even a few children.

Authorship is traditionally attributed to the Greek physician (or Hellenistic Jew) Luke, who appears to have used a number of existing oral and/or written accounts to compose and compile his work. This book is actually part one of a two-part compendium of the life of Jesus, the second part of which is the Book of Acts. Some conservative scholars suggest that Luke and Acts were composed under sponsorship of a sympathetic Roman authority named *Theophilos* (cf. Luke 1:1-4 and Acts 1:1) as part of the Apostle Paul's written testimony that would have been assembled in preparation for his trial in Rome before Caesar. A record of events surrounding Paul's trip to Rome is recorded in the second half of Acts.

Luke's Gospel has been symbolized as a man, representing the camp of Reuben standing south of the Tabernacle and serving as an expression of the character of the Messiah's brotherly sympathy with humanity by presenting Jesus as the fully human, loving friend, companion, associate, and leader.

The earliest possible date for the completion of Luke's Gospel must be the conclusion of events recorded in Acts 28, which records the Apostle Paul's arrest and two years of his captivity in Rome in the very early '60s AD. The second half of Luke's narrative history contains no concluding statement recording Paul's execution in Rome, which history records as having happened ca. 64 AD. Many conservative scholars surmise that Luke and Acts were completed shortly after the two year period noted in Acts 28:30 while Paul was still living. Otherwise, a notation would have been added regarding Paul's death in Rome to the end of the book of Acts.

The Messianic Theme is *The Gospel for Gentiles—Who Knew the Messiah?*

The Gospel of John

The *Gospel of John* refers to Mary without mentioning her by name during the instance of the wedding at Cana (John 2:1-12) and during the narrative of the crucifixion, where John describes her as standing near the cross of Jesus along with Mary Magdalene and Mary Cleophas in John 19:25-26.

This record of the life of Jesus is widely perceived as having been written to a largely Christian audience. Accordingly, this work focuses on the divine nature of Jesus, presenting him as the pre-existent, eternal Word of God who pitched his tent (as the literal Greek of John 1:14 records the event) for a time among the people whom he came to save. This work focuses on a number of "I AM" claims made by Jesus regarding his nature that link the identity, essential character, and nature of Jesus directly and unmistakably to the Name of God recorded in Exodus 3:14.

John's Gospel has been symbolized as an eagle, representing the camp of Dan standing north of the Tabernacle and serving as an expression of the character of the Messiah's soaring majesty by presenting him as the Word, God Himself in full, majestic, eternal, and all-powerful Deity and now permanently incarnate as a human being.

Early church tradition attributed this work to John, arguably one of the closest friends that Jesus maintained while in ministry. Highly developed and intricate claims portraying Jesus as both Messiah and as God incarnate are cited in John's narrative of what Jesus—and not merely John as the writer of this book—had to say about his nature and person, since the "I AM" statements are recorded as actual quotations from Jesus himself, not merely theological statements or conclusions about his nature. The early church father Irenaeus wrote that the Apostle John published this Gospel "during his residence at Ephesus in Asia" (*Against Heresies 3.1.1*).

Conservative scholars suggest that this work was completed well before the destruction of Jerusalem's Temple in 70 AD, since no mention is made about this momentous event within it. Speculation by non-conservative critics that this Gospel was composed as late as ca. 170 AD were refuted by discovery of the Roberts Fragment $\mathfrak{P}^{52}$, which contains parts of John 8:31-38, demonstrating that John's Gospel had gained enough history and wide-spread acceptance to have been circulated extensively by the early years of the second century AD, which in turns suggests that the Gospel of John had been complete for many decades before the beginning years of the second century AD.

The Messianic Theme is *The Gospel for Believers—Who is the Messiah?*

THE BOOK OF ACTS

The ***Book of Acts*** describes Mary and her sons as being gathered in the upper room after the Ascension of Jesus (Acts 1:14). This second half of the early proclamation of the Gospel is written to a largely gentile, but Christian audience. Traditionally attributed to the Greek physician (or Hellenistic Jew) Luke, who appears to have used a number of existing oral and/or written accounts to compose and compile his work, some conservative scholars theorize that Acts was composed under sponsorship of a sympathetic Roman authority named Theophilos (cf. Luke 1:1-4 and Acts 1:1) as part of the Apostle Paul's written testimony that would have been assembled in preparation for his trial in Rome before Caesar. A record of events surrounding Paul's trip to Rome is recorded in the second half of this book.

The earliest possible date for the completion of this book must be after the Apostle Paul's two years of captivity in Rome in the very early '60s AD. Because conservative scholars note that Acts contains no concluding narrative regarding Paul's execution in Rome, which happened ca. 64 AD, it is surmised that Acts must have been completed shortly after the two year period noted in Acts 28:30 while Paul was still living. Otherwise, a notation would have been added to the end of this book regarding Paul's death in Rome.

CONCLUDING THOUGHTS: ON THE VIRGINITY OF MARY

No study of the life of Mary, mother of Jesus, would be complete without addressing the various libelous allegations that have been lodged about her during the last 2,000 years. The main allegation that seems to have carried the most weight regarding Mary is the question of whether or not she was a virgin throughout her time of betrothal to Joseph. The *Talmud* is blunt in its accusation that Mary was an adulterer, as we've already noted, and as we'll comment again, below.

Irrespective of what various Church teachings may or may not have asserted with respect to Mary's post-betrothal years following her public marital vows, a plain reading of the text of the New Testament is clear and unequivocal in its pronouncement: Mary's pregnancy occurred *without* recourse to sexual involvement on any level with any human male antecedent to the actual birth of her son Jesus. The New Testament says that Mary was a virgin when she became pregnant with her son Jesus.

The enemies of Jesus denied this obviously supernatural event, but this denial would be expected, given the animosity that originated from the Pharisees, Sadducees, and the priestly leadership that ruled the Temple precincts with an iron hand, even if that hand was constantly tempered by the local Roman despots.

You can see evidence of the moral accusations against Mary and Jesus that followed them both throughout the public ministry of Jesus in John 8:41, where the Apostle John records the retort "We're not illegitimate children..." and which contains the unspoken accusation by the Jewish leaders, "...like you are!"

Even to the present day, the *Talmud* continues to transmit the profane tradition that Jesus, who is often referred to in that work by the anonymous moniker "So-and-So" was a *mamzer*, a Hebrew term that means an illegitimate child born out of wedlock from a fornicating wife's illicit sexual encounter with someone other than her marriage partner. Chilton summaries this view by saying:

> *What emerges from both Rabbinic literature (supplemented by Origen) and the New Testament is that Jesus' mother was clearly known and that the identity of his father was contested.*[12]

Furthermore, the clear and unmistakable claim of all of the records of the New Testament is that the conception of Jesus was a direct fulfillment of an ancient prophecy given by the Hebrew Scriptures prophet Isaiah, who wrote in Isaiah 7:14:

> [14]*Therefore the LORD himself will give you a sign. Watch! The virgin is conceiving a child, and will give birth to a son, and his name will be called Immanuel.*

The Dead Sea Scrolls edition of this verse claims that it was YHWH himself who provided the sign. The Masoretic Text, which dates about 1200 years later than Dead Sea Scrolls edition of Isaiah, has amended the text to read "Lord," using the Hebrew word *Adonai* instead of the Hebrew word for God. For those of our readers who are familiar with biblical Hebrew and Septuagint Greek, here is how this verse is rendered in those two biblical era scripts.

לָכֵן יִתֵּן אֲדֹנָי הוּא לָכֶם אוֹת הִנֵּה הָעַלְמָה הָרָה וְיֹלֶדֶת בֵּן וְקָרָאת שְׁמוֹ
עִמָּנוּ אֵל׃

---

12   For a fuller discussion of this blasphemous view, see Bruce Chilton's *The Mamzer Jesus and His Birth* cited at http://www.bibleinterp.com/articles/Chilton_Mamzer_Jesus_Birth.shtml.

[14]διὰ τοῦτο δώσει κύριος αὐτὸς ὑμῖν σημεῖον, ἰδοὺ ἡ παρθένος ἐν γαστρὶ ἕξει καὶ τέξεται υἱόν, καὶ καλέσεις τὸ ὄνομα αὐτοῦ Εμμανουηλ,[13]

The words highlighted in gray, above, may be translated as "the virgin" in Hebrew and Greek, respectively. Do note, if you would please, that the definite article exists in the text: the writer is referring to *"the* virgin"; i.e., to a specific person. As a footnote, the actual Hebrew literal translation of this verse into modern English reads:

> *The Lord himself will give them a sign: Look! The virgin will conceive and give birth to a son, and she will call his name "God with us."*

The Hebrew word "she will call" is a *feminine* singular future tense verb. It indicates that it shall be the mother who names the child. Traditionally, children were named by the father in Jewish culture, so for the prophet Isaiah to restrict the naming convention for Mary's son to his mother alone provides a not-so-sly hint that there was no human father present to claim the right of child naming.

Also, irrespective how modern liberal higher criticism has cast doubt as to whether or not the Hebrew word for *virgin* means "an unmarried woman of marital age" or a medically certifiable virgin, one thing is *abundantly clear* about the understanding of Joseph: *the man himself* assumed his betrothed wife was a virgin. *That's* why he was inclined to divorce her on fully biblical grounds when he discovered her pregnancy and why he was so upset when he learned she was pregnant before she and Joseph had celebrated the *Nasu'in* function of their marriage ceremony that we'll talk about in more detail on page 27: he *assumed* that virgins don't get pregnant!

Therefore Joseph logically assumed and concluded that Mary's growing baby bump provided *de facto* evidence that she had been unfaithful to him, her betrothed husband. Since the New Testament conveys the message that Mary *was discovered* (note the passive verb!) to be pregnant, it's clear from the sheer human drama of the

---

13 Septuaginta (Stuttgart: Deutsche Bibelgesellschaft, 1996), Is 7:14–15.

narrative that someone (perhaps Mary herself?) tried to suppress public knowledge of the pregnancy, but after a few months, the truth was made evident to anyone who had eyes to see.

At any rate, the New Testament records Joseph's intention to divorce Mary, and goes out of its way to note that he would have been righteous in doing so. It also records that God himself intervened by providing to Joseph an angelic visitation during a dream one night, which appearance would remind first century readers of the New Testament narrative of Daniel's angelic visitations recorded in that book of the Hebrew Scriptures. In that dream that Joseph received, he was informed about the heavenly realities involved in Mary's pregnancy.

ALMA VS. *BETULAH*: THE DEBATE ABOUT WHICH WORD MEANS *VIRGIN*

Throughout the years following the completion of the New Testament and the *Talmud* (the Jewish commentary on the Hebrew Scriptures that we mentioned in the section entitled Mary and Jesus in the Talmud on page 4), a debate has raged regarding what the true meaning of the Hebrew word *alma* in Isaiah is connoting. The Apostle Matthew clearly equates the virgin conception of Jesus by Mary as a fulfillment of Isaiah 7:14, which uses the word to describe the virginity of Mary. This is particularly relevant given that the Septuagint (the 2nd century BC Greek language translation of the Hebrew Scriptures made by Jewish scholars) renders the Hebrew word "virgin" with the Greek word παρθένος (*parthénos*), which unequivocally means "virgin," not "young woman."

But in later centuries, anti-missionary efforts by the Jewish community, coupled with the "scholarship" of various higher critics of the New Testament, have advanced the view that the word used by Isaiah 7:14 does not mean "virgin." Instead, these deniers of all things evangelical have suggested that the Hebrew word "betulah" means "virgin," instead. These critics conclude their arguments by suggesting that since Isaiah called the mother of the Messiah only a "young woman" of marriageable age (who in their view wasn't *necessarily* a virgin), and since Isaiah didn't called her a *betulah*, which in their view *does* mean *virgin*, Isaiah was not hinting at a virgin conception when he predicted Mary's pregnancy. As one observer summarized the argument:

> *Jewish revisers and naturalistic textual critics prefer to render almah as "young woman," hoping to undercut the prophetic value of the passage. They claim that if Isaiah were really desiring to prophesy that a virgin would conceive, that he would have used the Hebrew word bethulah, which is claimed as a more proper word for "virgin."*[14]

We have examined the relevant evidence and have concluded that the higher critics have the situation exactly *opposite* to the truth: that is, the Hebrew word *betulah* means a young woman, and not *necessarily* a virginal one, and that *alma* means a true virgin. For those of our readers who might be interested in the linguistic details regarding why we have reached this conclusion, we commend you to a careful reading of Appendix One, starting on page 181.

---

[14] For further reading, see http://www.studytoanswer.net/doctrine/almah.html, authored by Timothy W. Dunkin. The full text of this web page may be read as Appendix One to this work. It is reprinted there with the author's consent.

TEST #1:
ARE YOU WILLING TO
TRUST GOD WITH YOUR
WHOLE LIFE?

T he logical place to begin our study of the life of Mary, the mother of Jesus of Nazareth, is with one of the very first chronological instances in the New Testament where the young lady is mentioned. You'll find the narrative in the first chapter of the Gospel of Luke, the third biography of four such documents included at the very start of the New Testament records. In reading through this narrative regarding the life of Mary, we invite you to notice the following observations that we can glean from Mary's first spiritual challenge as to whether she will trust God with her whole life:

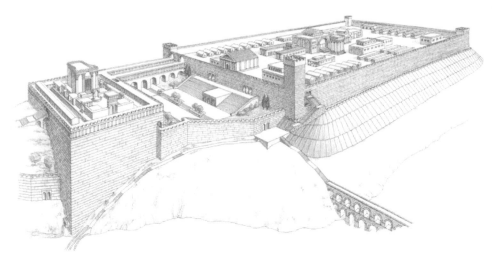

Figure 11: Temple showing City of David location.
Illustration pursuant to Ernest Martin

1. THE TIMING OF THE TEST: DIVINELY APPOINTED (LUKE 1:26)

We note that our first observation concerning Mary's first real test of her young life was that it took place during the sixth month of the pregnancy of Elizabeth, wife of the priest Zechariah and a close relative of Mary. Zechariah served in the Temple, which recent research indicates was located in the City of David about 200 yards south of the Antonia Fortress, the garrison that housed Rome's legions during the Roman Empire's occupation of ancient Israel. Earlier in the first chapter of Luke's Gospel, you can read the story of how Elizabeth had conceived her son John the Baptizer after her husband had received an angelic visitation during the one time of Zechariah's life that he had been chosen by lottery to offer incense in the Holy Place within that Temple. After his term of service had been completed, he returned to his residence. Elizabeth's pregnancy became evident shortly thereafter. The text of Luke 1:26 tells us that six months later, Mary received her first encounter with God's plan for her life:

> *²⁶Now in the sixth month of her pregnancy, the angel Gabriel was sent by God to a city in Galilee called Nazareth,...*

MARY'S ENGAGEMENT TO JOSEPH

In the theological and cultural economy of ancient Israel, young men were offered the opportunity to assume the responsibilities of adulthood voluntarily at the commencement of their twelfth year of age. Those responsibilities were mandatory at the commencement of the thirteenth year. By the time Mary was born c. 15 BC, this requirement had been applied to young girls, as well. The responsibilities involved for young women would include readiness for engagement, marriage, and child rearing (among other areas of application that aren't germane to our study). Accordingly, it's highly likely that Mary would not have been much older than thirteen years when she found herself engaged to Joseph. We must not be too dogmatic about this suggestion, however, since nothing in the text of the New Testament narratives informs us regarding her exact age at the time she became pregnant.

At any rate, under the Jewish cultural and religious traditions in full force and effect in Israel of that time, what we today call Mary's "engagement" to Joseph turns out to be a rather awkward and inaccurate translation of the Hebrew concept of the *kiddushin*, or betrothal. According to Jewish law, as a betrothed couple Joseph and Mary would legally be called "husband and wife," even though they were not yet living together under a single roof:

> *According to Torah law, marriage is a two-step process. The first stage is called "kiddushin," and the second step is known as "nisu'in." Kiddushin is commonly translated as betrothal, but actually renders the bride and groom full-fledged husband and wife. After this point, if, G-d forbid, they decided to part ways, a "get" (Jewish divorce) would be required. However, the bride and groom are not permitted to live together as husband and wife until the second stage, the nisu'in, is completed.*[1]

> *Under ancient Jewish tradition, the rabbis forbade betrothing through intercourse, making it a punishable offense. In order*

---

[1]   For a more detailed treatment of this subject, see http://www.chabad.org/library/article_cdo/aid/477321/
jewish/Kiddushin-Betrothal.htm.

for the betrothal to take effect, the transaction must be witnessed by two kosher witnesses. The common custom is to betroth by means of a money transaction, using the traditional wedding band to effect the kiddushin. ... The nisu'in is accomplished through "chupah"—the husband uniting with the wife under one roof for the sake of marriage. In ancient times, the two stages of marriage were done on separate occasions, often separated by a full year which the groom would devote to Torah study. Both the kiddushin and the nisu'in were accompanied by celebratory feasts.[2]

Alfred Edersheim comments regarding the specific situation in which Joseph and Mary would have been involved:

Whichever of the two modes of betrothal may have been adopted: in the presence of witnesses—either by solemn word of mouth, in due prescribed formality, with the added pledge of a piece of money, however small, or of money's worth for use; or else by writing (the so-called Shitre Erusin)—there would be no sumptuous feast to follow; and the ceremony would conclude with some such benediction as that afterwards in use: "Blessed art Thou, O Lord our God, King of the World, Who hath sanctified us by His Commandments, and enjoined us about incest, and forbidden the betrothed, but allowed us those wedded by Chuppah (the marriage-baldachino) and betrothal. Blessed art Thou, Who sanctifiest Israel by Chuppah and betrothal"—the whole being perhaps concluded by a benediction over the statutory cup of wine, which was tasted in turn by the betrothed. From that moment Mary was the betrothed wife of Joseph; their relationship as sacred, as if they had already been wedded. Any breach of it would be treated as adultery; nor could the bond be dissolved except, as after marriage, by regular divorce. Yet months might intervene between the betrothal and marriage.[3]

---

2   *Ibid.*
3   Alfred Edersheim, *The Life and Times of Jesus the Messiah*, vol. 1 (New York: Longmans, Green, and Co., 1896), 149–150.

SETTING THE BACKSTORY: ELIZABETH AND ZECHARIAH AS GOD'S LINKING HIS PAST WORK TO PRESENT ACTIVITY

As we'll note below, the first test that Mary would be facing in her young life is whether or not she was willing to trust God with her whole life. But before we can examine this episode, let's look at the backstory that precedes Mary's story. If you're familiar with God's pattern of work in the Old Testament, there's something about what Luke is telling us that is strangely familiar. Let's take a look at what Luke says in Luke 1:5-25:

> *⁵During the reign of King Herod of Judea, there was a priest named Zechariah, who belonged to the priestly order of Abijah. His wife was a descendant of Aaron, and her name was Elizabeth. ⁶Both of them were righteous before God, having lived blamelessly according to all of the commandments and regulations of the Lord. ⁷They had no children because Elizabeth was barren and because both of them were getting old.*

THE TWO WHO WILL COME

At this point of beginning of Luke's narrative of the life of Jesus the Messiah, the Hellenistic physician deliberately fashions his biography so that anyone who is familiar with the literary imagery of the Hebrew Scriptures cannot fail but notice that what God had done in ancient days he is beginning to do again. Biblical commentator Kenneth Litwak explains it this way:

> *Generally, when the Scriptures of Israel recount a birth annunciation, the child that is born played a significant role in God's purposes for Israel.*
> > • *Isaac (whose birth was announced in Genesis 18:10-15) was the beginning of the fulfillment of God's promise to Abraham.*
> > • *Samson (whose birth was announced and confirmed in Judges 13:3-20) helped deliver Israel from enslavement to the Philistines.*

- *Samuel (who was not born following a birth annunciation but whose birth is promised and recounted in 1 Samuel 1:12-20) provided the transition from judge to prophet as God's primary spokesperson, and he anointed and appointed the first two kings of Israel, Saul and David.*

By framing his discourse about the annunciations with these intertextual echoes of scriptural annunciation stories, Luke is telling his readers to interpret these annunciations as their predecessor accounts would be interpreted. Through them Luke tells his audience to understand the annunciations in his Gospel as relating to individuals who have a similarly important role in Israel, and in God's salvific purposes for his people. These two annunciations are not simply telling Luke's audience that two children will be born, using a common biblical style. These two annunciations, through Luke's discursive framing, tell his audience that God is showing his faithfulness to his people by working once again as he did in the Scriptures of Israel to bring deliverance and salvation to his people. By showing the connections between the past and present, the annunciations and their participants stand in continuity with those in Israel's past.[4]

Do notice, if you would please, that the pattern being displayed here isn't just a repeat of the rather remarkable tendency displayed by God in his ancient dealings with Israel to make little old ladies pregnant. There's something deeper at work here; specifically, the *continuation* by God of his work in the first century, AD, that he had brought to a revelatory conclusion in the mid-'400s, BC, at the end of the book of the prophet Malachi. Starting with this elderly couple named Zechariah and Elizabeth, God gets back to work, so to speak, on the fulfillment of his messianic promises.

And it's not that there weren't any general messianic expectations floating around the Jewish community of Roman-occupied *Palestinia*, either. As respected Biblical commentator H. A. Ironside puts it:

---

[4] Kenneth Duncan Litwak, *Echoes of Scripture in Luke-Acts: Telling the History of God's People Intertextually*, vol. 282, Journal for the Study of the New Testament Supplement Series (London; New York: T&T Clark International, 2005), 71.

There is an interval, as you know, of about four hundred years between the book of Malachi, the last book of the Old Testament, and the Gospels of the New Testament. We speak of these sometimes as "the four hundred silent years" because in those years we have no record, so far as inspired history is concerned, of God's speaking audibly to man, either directly Himself or through angelic ministration. Of course, in the books sometimes called "Apocrypha" we do read of angels visiting men and prophets being raised up, but in the inspired Scriptures we have no record of anything of the kind during those four hundred years. They were years of waiting. The people of Israel had returned from captivity in Babylon about B.C. 536 to 445. God had spoken to His prophet Daniel, saying that at the end of a certain limited period—483 years to be exact, 69 periods of seven years each—the Messiah was to come, and the people were waiting for His coming. They knew that the time had almost expired, and one can understand the expectancy with which the Jews would go up to Jerusalem year after year to keep the feasts of the Lord, hoping that the promise would be fulfilled.

But nothing happened until a never-to-be-forgotten day when a priest named Zacharias was ministering in the holy place in the temple at Jerusalem...[5]

Abijah's was the eighth of 24 priestly divisions set up by King David during his administration. You can read about those divisions in 1 Chronicles 24:1-19, where Abijah's name appears in verse 10:

[1]With respect to the descendants of Aaron, classes of service were organized for Nadab, Abihu, Eleazar, and Ithamar, the descendants of Aaron. [2]But Nadab and Abihu died before their father did, leaving no sons, so Eleazar and Ithamar became priests. [3]Along with Zadok, one of Eleazar's descendants,

---

5   H. A. Ironside, *Addresses on the Gospel of Luke*. (Neptune, NJ: Loizeaux Brothers, 1947), 20–21

and Ahimelech, one of Ithamar's descendants, David organized their service according to their assigned responsibilities.

⁴More leaders were located among Eleazar's descendants than among those of Ithamar, so sixteen leaders were appointed from the leaders of the ancestral households of Eleazar's descendants and eight from those of Ithamar. ⁵They were chosen by impartial lottery, since there were trustees of the sanctuary and officers of God among both Eleazar's descendants and among Ithamar's descendants. ⁶Nethanel's son Shemaiah, a Levitical scribe, made an official record of them for the king, the officers, Zadok the priest, Abiathar's son Ahimelech, and the heads of ancestral households of both the priests and the descendants of Levi. One ancestral house was chosen for Eleazar and one for Ithamar.

⁷The first lottery was chosen in favor of Jehoiarib, the second for Jedaiah, ⁸the third for Harim, the fourth for Seorim, ⁹the fifth for Malchijah, the sixth for Mijamin, ¹⁰the seventh for Hakkoz, the eighth for Abijah, ¹¹the ninth for Jeshua, the tenth for Shecaniah, ¹²the eleventh for Eliashib, the twelfth for Jakim, ¹³the thirteenth for Huppah, the fourteenth for Jeshebeab, ¹⁴the fifteenth for Bilgah, the sixteenth for Immer, ¹⁵the seventeenth for Hezir, the eighteenth for Happizzez, ¹⁶the nineteenth for Pethahiah, the twentieth for Jehezkel, ¹⁷the twenty-first for Jachin, the twenty-second for Gamul, ¹⁸the twenty-third for Delaiah, and the twenty-fourth for Maaziah. ¹⁹These were appointed to enter the Temple of the Lord according to their protocols established by their ancestor Aaron, as commanded by the Lord God of Israel.

Zechariah and Elizabeth: God's Pattern Continues

What Luke is relating to us in his narrative about Zechariah and Elizabeth is crafted by the writer in parallel with the other annunciation narratives that appear in the Hebrew Scriptures. Consider, for example, the expression "Don't be afraid!" It's common to God's annunciation narratives. The expression occurs frequently in the Septuagint, the Greek language translation of the Hebrew Scriptures produced during the mid-second century, BC.

- The angel of the Lord tells Hagar in Genesis 21:17 not to fear because God will take care of Ishmael.

- In Genesis. 26:1, God appears to Isaac and tells him not to fear.

- God says "Don't be afraid!" to Jacob when Jacob sees a vision of angels ascending into and descending from heaven in Genesis 28:13.

- In Judges 6:22-23, we read that Gideon saw the angel of the Lord and responded in anguish because he had seen the angel of the Lord face to face, which implies he feared for his safety because of this epiphany. The angel tells Gideon not to fear.

- In Daniel 10:12, 19, Daniel sees an angel in a great vision and is overcome. The angel may be Gabriel, whom Daniel has already encountered in Daniel 8:12; 9:21.

Luke is echoing the language and tradition of annunciations to pious, childless couples. Note the similarity of the language of Luke 1:7 to its predecessors in the Scriptures of Israel, specifically, Genesis 11:30; 18:11, and Judges 13:2. Specifically:

- These three accounts have several words in common, such as "barren," "child," or some similar cognate.

- Each couple was aged and childless.

- Annunciation stories in the Scriptures of Israel record the presence of the Angel of the Lord or similar figures.

- A common response to heavenly epiphany in annunciations is that the hearer is gripped with fear.

- This is followed by reassurance, also a common feature of heavenly epiphanies. The angel tells Zechariah not to fear, a clear echo of Genesis 15:1, intended to assure Zechariah that, like Abraham, God had not forgotten him.

ZECHARIAH AND THE MORNING SACRIFICE

Zechariah's appearance in the Holy Place within the main sanctuary of the Temple "was chosen by lot" (Luke 1:8). This observation by Luke is intended to remind his readers that what to outward, human appearances is a random choice by natural selection is, in fact, a divine appointment. Luke writes (Luke 1:8-10):

> *⁸When Zechariah was serving with his division of priests in God's presence, ⁹he was chosen by lot to go into the sanctuary of the Lord and burn incense, according to the custom of the priests. ¹⁰And the entire congregation of people was praying outside at the time when the incense was burned.*

Many modern commentators suggest that this incense offering was presented by Zechariah during the evening sacrifice because "the entire congregation of people was praying outside" when Zechariah's turn came to offer the sacrificial incense. There appears to be better evidence (as Alfred Edersheim proposes[6]) that the incense offering referred to by Luke occurred during the morning. Several competent observers of Hebrew worship customs suggest that the size of the priestly population at service during the first century limited a priest's time of incense offering to *once in a single lifetime of service.* If this view is correct, it is most instructive to observe what's on Zechariah's mind as he offers prayer and incense to God in the Holy Place. Luke 1:11-15a informs us:

> *¹¹An angel of the Lord appeared to him, standing at the right side of the incense altar. ¹²When Zechariah saw him, he was startled, and fear overwhelmed him. ¹³But the angel told him, "Stop being afraid, Zechariah, because your prayer has been heard. Your wife Elizabeth will bear you a son, and you are to name him John. ¹⁴You will have great joy, and many people will rejoice at his birth, ¹⁵because he will be great in the Lord's presence.*

---

6   Alfred Edersheim, *The Life and Times of Jesus the Messiah*, vol. 1 (New York: Longmans, Green, and Co., 1896), 133.

Succinctly stated, Zechariah uses the *one time in his professional life when he can talk directly to God in the Holy Place* to be thinking about his wife! Edersheim observes:

> *Only once in a lifetime might any one enjoy that privilege. Henceforth he was called "rich," and must leave to his brethren the hope of the distinction which had been granted him. It was fitting that, as the custom was, such lot should be preceded by prayer and confession of their faith on the part of the assembled priests. It was the first week in October 748 A.U.C.,[7] that is, in the sixth year before our present era, when "the course of Abijah"—the eighth in the original arrangement of the weekly service—was on duty in the Temple.[8]*

Then, in keeping with the very same annunciation patterns that we can read in the Hebrew Scriptures, Zechariah is given specific instructions as to how he is to raise his son. Luke 1:15b-17 sets forth those instructions, along with a statement regarding what God is going to do with his life:

> [15b]*He will never drink wine or any strong drink, and he will be filled with the Holy Spirit even before he is born.* [16]*He will bring many of Israel's descendants back to the Lord their God.* [17]*He is the one who will go before the Lord with the spirit and power of Elijah to turn the hearts of parents to their children and the disobedient to the wisdom of the righteous, and to prepare the people to be ready for the Lord."*

ZECHARIAH'S DOUBT

But Zechariah has his doubts. Luke 1:18 informs us…

> [18]*Then Zechariah asked the angel, "How can I be sure of this, since I am an old man, and my wife is getting older?"*

---

[7] This term 748 A.U.C. represents the Latin term *"Ab Urbe Condita"*; i.e., dating 748 years following the foundation of Rome in 753 BC.

[8] Alfred Edersheim, *The Life and Times of Jesus the Messiah*, vol. 1 (New York: Longmans, Green, and Co., 1896), 134–135.

Astonishingly, Zechariah's momentary response is *one of doubt.* He wonders how he can be sure that he's not being lied to. Note, please, how Zechariah isn't expressing *wonder* at the event. He doubts that God would single him out for his personal attention. As a result, Zechariah's doubt results in Gabriel responding with what we're tempted to call his own form of angelic wonder:

> [19] *The angel answered him, "I am Gabriel! I stand in the very presence of God. I have been sent to speak to you and to announce this good news to you.* [20] *But because you did not believe my announcement, which will be fulfilled at its proper time, you will become silent and unable to speak until the day this happens."*
>
> [21] *Meanwhile, the people kept waiting for Zechariah and wondering why he stayed in the sanctuary so long.* [22] *But when he did come out, he was unable to speak to them. Then they realized that he had seen a vision in the sanctuary. He kept motioning to them but remained unable to speak.* [23] *When the days of his service were over, he went home.*
>
> [24] *After this, his wife Elizabeth became pregnant and remained in seclusion for five months. She said,* [25] *"This is what the Lord did for me when he looked favorably on me and took away my public disgrace."*

THE PRIORITY OF PERSONAL TRUST IN THE GOD WHO HAS NO NEEDS

As we have noted, the first test that Mary faced is whether or not she was willing to trust God with her whole life. By presenting the necessity of answering that question, God would use this experience to prepare her to receive his best in a way that glorifies himself.

The Christian community has traditionally taught that God has no needs. He is sufficient and complete in himself, needing no external resources or influences to maintain the integrity of his person, nature, existence, his plans, and works. Nevertheless, in some mysterious way that no merely human being can completely understand, God appears to have interests. For example, in Philippians 2:21, the Apostle complains to his Christian readers that "…all the others look after their own interests, not after those of Jesus the Messiah." This statement clearly implies that God in the incarnation of Jesus as the Messiah has personal interests. He has things he wants to accomplish in the world, and he wants to use his people to fulfill them:

- His long-term goal is to glorify himself by exalting his Son, the Lord Jesus the Messiah.

- His mid-range objective is to multiply disciples, which he intends to accomplish by sending his followers throughout the world to spread the good news that God in the Messiah has reconciled to himself everyone who places their trust in him.

- The day-to-day missions that he wants accomplished include a faith in him on the part of his followers that work in the daily world to visit those in prison, to feed the poor, clothe the naked, and minister to those who are suffering.

It appears that the single most significant interest God has in relationship to his people is his desire for them to trust him completely and implicitly. One of the best examples of this desire on the part of God for his people to trust him with the sum and substance of their lives is seen in the life of Mary, the mother of Jesus the Messiah.

In an essay written by political pundit and analyst Kirsten Powers and published on 17 December 2015 by *Christianity Today*, Ms. Powers observed:

At every turn in the story of Christmas we witness unquestioning obedience to God. A young virgin is told she will conceive a son by the Holy Spirit. How will she explain this to her husband-to-be? What if he refuses to marry her and she's left to bear a son out of wedlock? These were not minor concerns in the time in which she lived. Still, her response to the angel Gabriel is profound in its simplicity. "I am the Lord's servant," Mary says. "May your word to me be fulfilled." How many of us are slower to respond to God's prompting over much smaller matters?

Joseph was just as quick to ignore his worldly concerns and acquiesce to the call of God. Upon learning the news of Mary's pregnancy, he decided to quietly end the engagement so as to not expose her to public disgrace. But mercifully, he, too, had a dream. An angel of the Lord appeared to him and told him to "not be afraid" to take Mary as his wife. He obeyed. And then he and Mary joined in their obedience to welcome into the world the Light of all mankind.[9]

Ms. Powers is correct in her observations, especially when she asked the not-so-rhetorical question, "How many of us are slower to respond to God's prompting over much smaller matters?" And that question summarizes in a single sentence the important role that Mary plays in the New Testament: God wants to be trusted, and Mary's life is an example of how that trust works in the life of God's people. Of the ten test questions that God puts to Mary throughout the course of her life, she manages to pass nine of them with flying colors. Receiving a test score of 90-95%, as the record of the New Testament reports, is a spectacular achievement, indeed.

2. THE MEANS OF THE TEST: THROUGH GOD'S MESSENGER (LUKE 1:27)

The second observation we can glean from Matthew's narrative that presents Mary's first major challenge to her spiritual life concerns the means by which that challenge was presented. Luke 1:26 tells us that the angel Gabriel was sent by God to visit her. We invite you to note what Luke tells us happened next. Luke 1:27 tells us that Gabriel was sent:

[27]...to a virgin engaged to a man named Joseph, a descendant of David. The virgin's name was Mary.

9 "Becoming a Christian Ruined My Love of Christmas". Cited from http://www.christianitytoday.com/ct/2015/december-web-only/kirsten-powers-becoming-christian-ruined-my-love-of-christm.html.

Figure 12: Modern Nazareth and view of the Basilica of the Annunciation, commemorating Gabriel's appearance to Mary.
Image source: https://upload.wikimedia.org/wikipedia/commons/d/d5/Nazareth_the_ magical_city_111.jpg

We're not told much about Gabriel in Scripture. He appears to be tasked with the presentation of divine announcements on behalf of God's people. It was Gabriel who visited Zechariah to inform him that his prayers had been answered concerning his wife Elizabeth. Both of them were elderly, and they had no children. Since Zechariah's opportunity to present prayers and

Figure 13: Modern Nazareth, viewed from the South.

Figure 14: Modern Nazareth, viewed from the North.

Figure 15: Map of first century Israel showing location of Nazareth east of Mount Carmel and west of Tiberias.

incense in the Holy Place was appointed by lottery only, and even then only *once* in the offeror's lifetime, Zechariah had used this exclusive and unique time of personal prayer to ask God for favor on behalf of his wife. Gabriel's visit to inform Zechariah of the pending pregnancy of his wife with the person who would become John the Baptizer was God's response to Zechariah's unselfish prayer on her behalf.

WHEN GOD MAKES A HOUSE CALL (LUKE 1:27)

Luke 1:26 succinctly tells us that Mary's first spiritual test took place right in her own home town. He writes of Gabriel's visit "to a city in Galilee called Nazareth." Nazareth exists to this day. Mount Carmel lays almost directly west of Nazareth, overlooking the Mediterranean Sea. The western shore of the Sea of Galilee lies directly east of Nazareth. Mary lived there with her parents and siblings, if she had siblings. (The Bible never mentions her brothers or sisters, though it's highly probable that she had them.) God sent Gabriel to meet Mary where she lived, in her own house. One practical principle we can learn from the circumstances of this first test is that God is willing and able to meet us where we live, in the here and now. No monastic withdrawal to distant places is necessary to encounter him and his plans for our lives. In simple terms, we don't have to go to pious retreats, out-of-the-way locations, or exotic locales away from others in order to learn what God has in store for us. He can meet us right where we live, even in the midst of the distractions of family and other life responsibilities.

And when he does meet us, we learn that life isn't linear. It can change course in a moment of time. What was our lot in life in the morning as we begin our day can easily shift focus so that by the afternoon, the most unimaginable things can happen that will change our life forever.

For Mary of Nazareth, the unimaginable came to visit on what started out as a quiet morning and changed radically in a moment of time when God engaged in a personal house call to a thirteen year old young girl who lived in a small town just a little bit down the road, north of Jerusalem.

3. THE ANNOUNCEMENT OF THE TEST: TO GOD'S CHOSEN WOMAN (LUKE 1:28-30)

The third observation we can make about Mary's first spiritual test concerns the nature of God's choice of Mary. Specifically, God has no volunteers. Luke writes in Luke 28-30:

> *[28] The angel came to her and said, "Greetings, you who are highly favored! The Lord is with you!" [29] Startled by his statement, she tried to figure out what his greeting meant. [30] Then the angel told her, "Stop being afraid, Mary, because you have found favor with God.*

He is the initiator of discipleship. God calls, and we are invited to respond. About the only possible exception to this pattern may be seen when God asked the not-so-rhetorical question, "Whom will I send? Who will go for us?" in Isaiah 6:8. To this inquiry, the prophet Isaiah replied, "Here I am!" .... "Send me." In the days of his mortality, the Lord Jesus was approached by a volunteer, who offered to become his disciple. You can read the story in Luke 10:17-22, where we read:

> *[17] As Jesus was setting out again, a man ran up to him, knelt down in front of him, and asked him, "Good Teacher, what must I do to inherit eternal life?"*
> *[18] "Why do you call me good?" Jesus asked him. "Nobody is good except for one—God. [19] You know the commandments:*

'Never murder.' 'Never commit adultery.' 'Never steal.'
'Never give false testimony.' 'Never cheat.' 'Honor your father
and mother.'"
[20]The man replied to him, "Teacher, I have obeyed all of these
since I was a young man."
[21]Jesus looked at him and loved him. Then he told him,
"You're missing one thing. Go and sell everything you own,
give the money to the destitute, and you will have treasure
in heaven. Then come back and follow me." [22]Shocked at
this statement, the man went away sad, because he had
many possessions.

Jesus set the standard so high for the wealthy young aristocrat who had stepped forward that the man rejected the requirements set forth by Jesus. It never occurred to this young man that if he had obeyed the conditions set by Jesus for becoming his disciple, Jesus himself would have provided the power to meet the expectations that he had for the man. Instead, the aristocrat walked away, disappointed because in his limited view of life, the cost of discipleship was too high to pay. In the case of Mary, God's *prevenient grace* went ahead of her, preparing her temperament, personality, and life situations ahead of time so that when his call came to her, that call would not be ineffective.

Furthermore, let's make no mistake about the dynamics of God's calling—thirteen years old is old enough to assume the responsibilities of walking straight into God's plan for your life. What the modern person today might think is much too young to contemplate the things of God, the Bible makes it clear that even young people can be chosen by God.

Mary wasn't the first person in history to have been set aside from their youth for participation in God's calling and covenant. Joseph was just a young teenager when he first had dreams about what God had in store for his life. Jacob was called to participate in God's covenant before he was even born. Samuel was called to ministry while still a child. Daniel resolved to love and follow God while still a young man in training for service in Nebuchadnezzar's administration. John the Baptizer was filled with the Holy Spirit, after the manner of the Old Testament prophets, while still in his pre-natal state.

Now with respect to Mary, given the outworking of God's plan for all of humanity, Matthew makes it clear to us in Matthew 1:27 that Gabriel's visit was "…to a virgin engaged to a man named Joseph, a descendant of David. The virgin's name was Mary." And so God's prevenient favor goes before Mary, preparing her for the most startling announcement any human being has ever received:

> *²⁸The angel came to her and said, "Greetings, you who are highly favored! The Lord is with you!"*

Frankly, it's no wonder that this statement turned her thirteenth year of life in this world upside down:

> *²⁹Startled by his statement, she tried to figure out what his greeting meant.*

We'd like to suggest that the words contained in the angel's announcement weren't, strictly speaking, what surprised Mary. Frankly, the greeting from the angel had a generic application that pertains to *any* person of faith. God is *always* present with his people. His favor always rests on those whom God has chosen.

No, we submit that what startled Mary wasn't the words themselves *per se*. We think what startled her was the surprising revelation that God had decided to have the message delivered to her and reinforced to her *personally*. Despite what you read in the modern "Evangelical-lite" books about angels that are being published nowadays, angels aren't in the habit of communicating with human beings. Frankly, there's a reason why the Bible calls them "watchers" or "observers": they don't normally interact with human beings in a way that the objects of their attention are aware of directly.

Mary was intelligent enough to recover her wits quickly, despite the initial fear of receiving a visit from an emissary directly from the throne of God. Bluntly put, Gabriel's statement contained nothing about God's care for her that she didn't already know. Or so she thought. The *really* startling part, however, was yet to come. And this startling part brings us to our next observation regarding the first spiritual test of her young life.

4. THE PURPOSE OF THE TEST: GOD'S CHARTER FOR HUMANITY (LUKE 1:31-33)

Mary was being asked the question, "Will you trust God with your whole life?" In addition to what God had in mind for her personal life, there was something going on that was so momentous, so critically important to the human race that a divine announcement was called for. In Luke 1:31, the angel interrupts her contemplation with the blunt command "Listen!" You'll find that the Greek term found here (ἰδού, *idoù*) is used by the speaker as an attention getting device, indicating to the hearer that something radical is coming, and that you'd do well to pay attention, since life is going to get rather complicated very, very quickly. The angel continues with his announcement by telling Mary:

> [31] *You will become pregnant and give birth to a son, and you are to name him Jesus.*

Gabriel's pronouncement consisted of two parts, a short term agenda and a long term objective. The short term agenda had to do with God's immediate purposes for Mary: she would become pregnant,[10] give birth to a son, and name her child in keeping with that child's divine nature and character. She was instructed to name him "Jesus," which in the Hebrew language meant "The LORD saves." That the instruction specifically required Mary to name the child, and not Mary and Joseph together, is a not-so-subtle hint that Joseph was to have no naming rights to the son, since (as Mary will shortly observe) Joseph will not have been the father of the child.

---

10   The Greek word used in Luke 1:31 and translated as "you will become pregnant" (συλλήμψῃ, *sullémpsē*) is a somewhat grammatically awkward use of the rare *Koiné* Greek word συλλαμβάνω (*sullambánō*). It's a second person singular infinitive, future indicative middle voice form of the verb. Strictly speaking the verb means "to take part in." We note that the middle voice here seems to imply no active participation by Mary in the conception. See our further comments, below, about how the Spirit of God was to do all the work of making the conception occur without human involvement on any level.

God's long term agenda must have been almost incredible to Mary. Almost, but not quite, since Mary will respond immediately with humble obedience to God's calling. Do note, if you would, how far reaching the plan of God for Mary's life was to be:

> *[32] He will be great and will be called the Son of the Most High…*

This statement by Gabriel to Mary is an explicit claim that the child who will be born to her shares the characteristics of divinity. By calling Jesus "the Son of the Most High," the angel is not saying that the Son of God will begin his existence at birth, just as a father pre-exists the son whom he begets. This false teachings is promulgated by aberrant, cultic groups such as the Jehovah's Witnesses, the Mormons, and other groups that deny the eternal divinity of Jesus.

In contrast to this, the angel Gabriel is referring to the Jewish view that a man's son shares the characteristics of his father. In the cultural and theological economy of first century Israel, since the term "the Most High" was a polite and respectful euphemism for God himself, and since Gabriel tells Mary that Jesus "will be great," the angel is declaring that the seed of Mary will be both fully human and fully divine. But there's more in store for Mary. Gabriel also announces:

> *…and the Lord God will give him the throne of his ancestor David. [33] He will rule over the house of Jacob forever, and his kingdom will never end."*

At this point, let's pause for a moment and contemplate the main aspect of Gabriel's statement that many of us miss as we read the Gospel account recorded by Matthew. That main aspect is this: *nothing* in the statement we've just quoted came to pass in Mary's lifetime. Consider, if you would, the following points:

- The giving over to Jesus by God of David's throne was not something that Mary could have observed. Messiah sitting on the throne of David will not occur until the Millennial Kingdom begins, and Mary did not have the benefit of our

45

viewpoint today that looks back over the last 2,000 years of history to understand this concept.

- Jesus never ruled over the house of Jacob during Mary's lifetime. Except for Pilate's prescient order to affix a sign that read "Jesus of Nazareth, King of the Jews" on the cross, nobody recognized him as the rightful heir to the throne of David, except those to whom this rare insight was given.

- The only part of Jesus' kingdom that Mary ever saw with her own eyes was the beginning years of the Church that he would establish.

What Gabriel is talking about looks far beyond Mary's life and takes into account the very purpose for which humanity was created. King David understood this amazing fact. In 2 Samuel 7:18-29, when presented with God's promise to establish his kingdom forever, King David:

> *[18]...went in to the presence of the LORD, sat down, and said: "Who am I, Lord GOD, and what is my family, that you have brought me to this? [19]And this is still a small thing to you, Lord GOD—you also have spoken about the future of your servant's house, and this is the charter for mankind, O Lord GOD!"*
> *[20]"What more can David say to you, and you surely know your servant, Lord GOD. [21]For the sake of your word and consistent with your desire, you have done all of these great things, informing your servant. [22]And therefore you are great, Lord GOD, there is no one like you, there is no God except for you, just as we've heard with our own ears.*
> *[23]"And who is like your people, like Israel, the one nation on earth that God went out to redeem as a people for himself, to make a name for himself, and to carry out for them great and awe-inspiring accomplishments, driving out nations and their gods in front of your people, whom you redeemed to yourself from Egypt? [24]You have prepared your people Israel to be*

your very own people forever, and you, LORD, have become their God!
[25]"And now, Lord GOD, let what you have spoken concerning your servant and his household be done—and let it be done just as you've promised. [26]May your name be made great forever with the result that it is said that the LORD of the Heavenly Armies is God over Israel, and that the household of your servant David may be established before you. [27]For you, LORD of the Heavenly Armies, the God of Israel, have revealed this to your servant, telling him, 'I will build a dynasty for you,' so that your servant has found fortitude to pray this prayer to you.
[28]"Now therefore, Lord GOD, you are God, and your words are true, and you have spoken to your servant these good things. [29]So may it please you to bless the household of your servant, so that it might remain forever in your presence, because you, Lord GOD, have spoken, and from your blessing may the household of your servant be blessed forever."

In light of David's pronouncement, it's pretty clear that Mary was standing at the very same crossroads of humanity's history that David experienced. In David's case, David was looking at the beginning of God's plan for his life. In Mary's case, Mary was doing the exact same thing, and she responded with the very same faith that David displayed. She consented to be part of what God was getting ready to do.

MARY: THE TEENAGER WHO COOPERATED WITH GOD'S PLAN

While God initiated his plans for Mary's life, Mary herself had a responsibility to respond by cooperating with what he intended to do. The resulting pregnancy that would come about was no act of forceful invasion of her life. Bluntly stated, *her pregnancy was fully consensual* in all respects. Anyone who claims otherwise is ignorant of the plain text of the New Testament record.

Not everyone holds this view. For example, self-styled "free thinker" Marcel Cagné wrote in a personal weblog as follows:

> *I was drawn to thinking about the most famous case of rape in the Bible, the rape of Mary, mother of Jesus. Technically, she was just a girl, so in our modern Western world, forcing a 14 year old girl to give birth to your baby is statutory rape. But these were dark times, well before satellite television or the Internet. There were lots of 14 year old mothers around.*

> *Still, Mary was betrothed to Joseph when God came calling. Did Mary's body know it had been raped? You would think it didn't because her body still got pregnant & gave birth to Jesus. So, in the logic of Akin, it wasn't a **legitimate** rape. I'm saying it had to have been rape because Mary didn't have a choice in the matter. Did she really have the opportunity to refuse? Could she? ...*

> *Some of you will argue that the above passage does seem to imply consent, but was it really that way? Mary knew it was God who was about to have sex with her, perhaps she felt she had no choice. Victims have been known to comply for fear of being beaten or killed and Yahweh had a long history of violence. She may well have known that saying no to God was pretty much a death sentence and so she complied, cheated on her husband-to-be and did what she was told.*

> *So it could have been rape. Just not legitimate rape.*[11]

In late October 2012, Richard Mourdock, a Republican senatorial candidate, made media headlines when:

> *...he argued that, if you really stop to think about it, the Virgin Mary was basically raped by God. "Mary certainly didn't ask for God to impregnate her with our Lord and Savior Jesus Christ, but obviously the Immaculate Conception, while not the result of a consensual act, was still a part of God's plan—you see what*

---

11 Cited from http://www.marcelgagne.com/content/rape-mary-legitimate-or-not.

I'm getting at, right?" said the 61-year-old man who currently serves as the state treasurer of Indiana.

Let us ignore for the moment Mourdock's obvious ignorance of even the most elementary terms of a Biblical theology concerning the Incarnation. (The man displays a sophomoric confusion of the term "Immaculate Conception," which deals with the Catholic dogma that *Mary* was conceived sinless, with the traditional Christian view of the virgin conception by Mary, which states that *Jesus* was conceived without resort to the role of a human father.) Mourdock continued:

"Of course I don't condone sexual assault. I'm just saying that sometimes when a woman is violated and impregnated against her will, it's actually a really good thing in the end, because God's rape of Mary gave us Jesus, and Jesus saved mankind from sin. So that's one example right there." At press time, multiple male Senate candidates in their 60s remained divided between those who believe pregnancies resulting from rape are biologically impossible and those who believe they are the divine will of God.[12]

The Bible is clear on the subject. Mary was not raped by God. She was chosen by divine will and the young lady considered her having been singled out by God as the highest of human privileges. So she obediently acquiesced to the announcement with full cooperation.

5. THE DESIGN OF GOD'S TEST—WHEN GOD DOES THE IMPOSSIBLE (LUKE 1:34-37)

There's a difference between unbelief and simple curiosity. When presented with God's plan to have Zechariah and his wife Elizabeth bear a child in their old age who would become John the Baptizer, Zechariah responded by asking "How can I be sure of this, since I am an old man, and my wife is getting older?" (Luke 1:18) In contrast to Zechariah's inquiry, which contained within it an outright claim of skepticism, Mary asked an innocent

---

[12] Cited from http://www.theonion.com/article/mother-mary-was-essentially-raped-mourdock-says-wh-30083.

question concerning *how* the promise would be fulfilled, given that she was committed to pre-marital purity and moral excellence:

> [34]*Mary asked the angel, "How can this happen, since I have not had relations with a man?"*

In simple terms, whereas Zechariah expressed *doubt*, Mary expressed *wonderment*. While both were initially startled by their angelic visitation, where Zechariah was skeptical, Mary was merely curious. Zechariah's questioning response led to a short season of discipline that did not affect the ultimate fulfillment of God's promise to this elderly couple, while Mary's faithful response led God to respond through the angel Gabriel with as complete and honest an answer that merely human intellect could comprehend:

> [35]*The angel answered her, "The Holy Spirit will come over you, and the power of the Most High will surround you.*

God Meets Mary within the Limits of her own Limited Understanding

Notice, if you would, how the angel Gabriel meets Mary at the exact location of her limited human understanding. The first century BC was not an era of scientific knowledge in which God could have provided a detailed explanation of DNA, fetal cell development, and other modern aspects of the science involved in conceiving a human male without the benefit of a father. Even if Mary had possessed a knowledge of human conception commensurate with modern understanding, the bottom line of that understanding is that *parthenogenesis* (i.e., *virgin conception*, a process that is known today to occur in lower life forms such as frogs) *cannot produce male offspring.*

A woman's reproductive system produces only female chromosomes. The father's contribution to the pregnancy supplies the male chromosomes necessary to produce a male. What Gabriel is telling Mary, within the limits of the young lady's own understanding, is that God is going to overrule the normal by intercepting the natural process, intervening with his supernatural power that will overrule nature to craft a one-time miracle. As a result, Gabriel tells Mary:

> *Therefore, the child will be holy and will be called the Son of God. ³⁶And listen! Elizabeth, your relative, has herself conceived a son in her old age, this woman who was rumored to be barren is in her sixth month. ³⁷Nothing is impossible with respect to any of God's promises."*

This last statement that nothing is impossible with respect to any of God's promises is not merely a statement of fact, it's a *personal* testimony by the angel Gabriel of the faithfulness and omnipotence of God to carry out everything that he proposes to do.

6. THE NECESSITY OF A RESPONSE FROM MARY (LUKE 1:38)

When you add up the sum of what it means to walk with God, belief in him may be defined as *cooperating with God regarding what he has already decided to do.* It's not a matter of intellectual understanding or belief, though God doesn't mind us asking honest questions. Honest questions can be supplied with honest answers that comply with our limited understanding.

With respect to Mary's first spiritual test of her young life, what was really at stake was her willingness to let God control her entire future. And, in her case at least, he was inviting her to be pivotal part in the future work of God on earth. Notice, if you would, how Mary's short response parallels what King David had said to God about a thousand years earlier when God promised to send his incarnate Messiah through David's lineage one day in the future:

> ³⁸*Then Mary said, "Truly I am the Lord's servant. Let everything you have said happen to me." Then the angel left her.*

As I've read this verse in the past, I've often wondered whether she fully understood the implications of what she had agreed to be a part of when she said "Yes" to God. For example, we invite the reader to take a good, close look at how Joseph responded to the news of Mary's out-of-wedlock pregnancy, as Matthew tells the story in Matthew 1:18-25:

> *[18]Now the birth of Jesus the Messiah happened in this way. When his mother Mary was engaged to Joseph, before they lived together she was discovered to be pregnant by the Holy Spirit.*

Please observe a couple of nuances that are discernible in this narrative. *First,* notice the oblique reference to the *passive voice* concerning the news of Mary's pregnancy: verse 18 describes her as having been "discovered to be pregnant…" Does this verse mean to imply or suggest that for a season Mary *was embarrassed* to be seen in her condition antecedent to her having moved in with Joseph? Notice how Joseph reacted, initially at first, to the news:

> *[19]Her husband Joseph, being a righteous man and unwilling to disgrace her, decided to divorce her secretly.*

JOSEPH'S UTTERLY NATURAL REACTION TO MARY'S CONDITION

At this point, we can make our second observation about Joseph: this the obvious and self-evident conclusion that Joseph (nor Mary, for that matter) held no illusions about how young women become pregnant. Joseph rightly concluded that he had become engaged to a woman who had become morally unfaithful to God and to him. But he decided to act within the context of gracious righteousness and not subject her to the penalty of reserved for adulterers under Israel's law. That penalty could have been as egregious as her being stoned to death at one extreme, or as simple as issuing a quiet *get,* a written decree of Jewish divorce. Joseph decided on the latter solution to his and Mary's vexing problem. But God had other plans:

> *[20]After he had thought about it, an angel of the Lord appeared to him in a dream. "Joseph, son of David," he said, "don't be afraid to take Mary as your wife, because what has been conceived in her is from the Holy Spirit. [21]She will give birth to a son, and you are to name him Jesus, because he is the one who will save his people from their sins."*

²²Now all this happened to fulfill what was declared by the Lord through the prophet when he said,
²³"See, a virgin will become pregnant
and give birth to a son,
and they will name him Immanuel,"
which means, "God with us."
²⁴When Joseph got up from his sleep, he did as the angel of the Lord had commanded him and took Mary as his wife. ²⁵He did not have marital relations with her until she had given birth to a son; and he named him Jesus.

CONCLUSION: THE GOD WHO LOVES TO ACCOMPLISH THE IMPOSSIBLE...

It's evident from Mary's response to the angelic invitation to become mother of the Messiah that she was willing to raise Jesus as an unmarried parent if that's what it would take to be at the center of God's will. By grace, since both Mary *and* Joseph were righteous individuals, God supernaturally intervened in order to provide providential direction and instructions to Joseph, encouraging him to conquer the fears that he harbored in his heart about what might come from his friends and relatives thinking that his wife was an unfaithful adulterer. He married Mary soon afterward.

Now if you're still having trouble grasping the concept of the Incarnation, as to how and why God should become man, we commend you to two things:

- *First,* keep in mind that the thing was thought to be impossible by both *Mary* and *Joseph* absent a divine revelation.

- Mary was so confused that she asked the angel how the thing would happen.

- Joseph was hurt, angry, and confused as to what to do, on the pragmatically simple grounds that he hadn't been brought into the information loop by God. So he received an angelic visitation in a dream and his security clearance, so to speak, was upgraded for the sake of Mary.

- And *second*, if you're still looking for insights regarding this mystery, you might do well to consider taking a good look at the writings of the 11th century abbot of Bec, who is commonly referred to as St. Anselm. Anselm writes in Book Two, letter #8 of his classic work *Cur Deus Homo* (Latin for *Why the God-Man?*) as follows:

Now let's examine whether the human nature taken by God must be produced from a father and mother, as other men are, or from man alone, or from woman alone. Obviously, it's going to be from one of these three possibilities, so that either way, this human will have been produced from Adam and Eve, since every person of either sex descended from these two people. Now as to these three modes, neither one is easier or more difficult for God than another, that it should be selected on this account. ...

Think about this: it's no big deal to show that the union of human and divine will be brought into existence in a nobler and purer manner, if this being is produced from man alone, or woman alone, than if the union comes about springing from the union of both a man and a woman, as is the case with all other human beings. ...

Therefore the one who is to make atonement must be taken either from man alone, or woman alone. ...

Actually, there are four possible ways by which God can create man:
  - *First, either from a man and a woman, in the common way; or*
  - *Second, neither from a man nor a woman, as he created Adam; or*
  - *Third, from a man without a woman, which he had already done before when God made Eve; or*
  - *Fourth, from a woman without a man, which until Jesus came he had never done.*

Well now, God already had worked the first three options. Therefore, in order to show that this last mode was also under his power (and was reserved for this very purpose!) what could be more fitting than that he should take that man whose origin we are seeking from a woman without using a man to do it? Now whether it be more worthy that the God-man be born of a virgin, or one not a virgin, we need not discuss, but must affirm, beyond all doubt, that the God-man should be born of a virgin. ...

Does what we have said appear sound, or does our argument seem like we're just blowing smoke...?

...Well then, let's build our foundation on solid truth. Let's remember how fitting it is that, just as man's sin and the cause of our condemnation sprung from a woman, so the cure of sin and the source of our salvation should also be found in a woman. Here's something else to consider: so that women may not despair of attaining the inheritance of the blessed, because that so dire an evil arose from woman, it is proper that from a woman also so great a blessing should arise, that their hopes may be revived.

Think about this, too. If it was a virgin who brought evil upon the race, it is much more appropriate that a virgin should be the occasion of all sorts of good. And also think about this: If woman, whom God made from man alone, was made from a virgin man (i.e., Adam), it is particularly fitting, is it not, that this new Man also, who shall spring from a woman, be born from a woman without a man? These explanations demonstrate the propriety of the God-man needing to be born from a virgin. These arguments should be sufficient for most inquirers.[13]

---

13 Cited from this writer's *Anselm Writes Again*. (Bellflower, CA: ISV Foundation, 2014), a modern retelling of St. Anselm's *Cur Deus Homo*, Book Two, Blog Post #8. Anselm provides a brilliant explanation for what the Apostle Paul says about Eve's role in the redemption of fallen man in 1 Timothy 2:13-15:

> [13]*For Adam was formed first, then Eve,* [14]*and it was not Adam who was deceived. It was the woman who was deceived and became disobedient,* [15]*even though she will be saved through the birth of the Child, if they continue in faith, love, and holiness, along with good judgment.*

For the Apostle Paul, woman's role in formal redemptive ministry was complete in the Virgin conception of Jesus the Messiah. Hence woman's *exemption* from the requirement and obligation of priestly service to the larger community of faith.

ELIZABETH GREETS THE MOTHER OF HER LORD

About six months after Zechariah's visit from the angel Gabriel, Mary paid a house call on her close relative. Luke describes the event in Luke 1:39-45:

> *³⁹Later on, Mary set out for a Judean city in the hill country. ⁴⁰She went into Zechariah's home and greeted Elizabeth. ⁴¹When Elizabeth heard Mary's greeting, the baby jumped in her womb. Elizabeth was filled with the Holy Spirit ⁴²and she loudly exclaimed, "How blessed are you among women, and how blessed is the infant in your womb! ⁴³Why should this happen to me, to have the mother of my Lord visit me? ⁴⁴As soon as the sound of your greeting reached my ears, the baby in my womb jumped for joy. ⁴⁵How blessed is this woman who believed that what the Lord told her would be fulfilled!"*

The physician makes two remarkable observations regarding Elizabeth. Given his medical training, we find it significant that Luke claims that this expectant mother knew instinctively what her as yet unborn son was feeling, because she tells Mary that he "jumped for joy" in her womb. She also knew that Mary was already pregnant, since she addressed Mary as the mother of her Lord, thus indicating both that she knew Mary was expecting and also that she recognized the divine nature of the child Mary was already carrying. At this point, Elizabeth is about six months pregnant, and Mary is somewhere between four to perhaps as much as six weeks along in her own pregnancy.

THE MAGNIFICAT

Theologians throughout Church history have referred to Mary's prophetic song that follows Elizabeth's greeting as *The Magnificat*. This is a Latin term that means "*Magnifies,*" and comes from the first word of the hymn in the Latin Vulgate translation of Luke's Gospel (which was originally written in Koiné Greek. The subject of the verb ("My soul") and the object of the verb ("the Lord") is added to the hymn by tradition so that the title of the song may rightly be translated into English as "My soul magnifies the Lord". Mary's song is one of four Judeo-Christian hymns that have been handed down to us by virtue of them being recorded in Luke's Gospel. The four hymns are:

- Zechariah's hymn of blessing, commonly called *The Benedictus*, recorded in Luke 1:67-79; and,

- Mary's *Magnificat* recorded in Luke 2:46-55; and,

- The *Gloria in Excelsis* uttered by the angels at their announcement of the Messiah's birth in Bethlehem recorded in Luke 2:13-14; and,

- Simeon's *Nunc Dimittis* recorded in Luke 2:28-32.

It's clear from reading through the structure of *The Magnificat* (as well as the other three hymns) that all four songs are rooted in the literary genre of the Psalms. The structure of *The Magnificat* is particularly evident as being crafted as *poetry* containing characteristic synonymous parallelism features beginning with the very first two lines of Mary's hymn:

⁴⁶Then Mary said,
"My soul praises the greatness of the Lord!
⁴⁷My spirit exults in God, my Savior,

We invite the reader to note, if you would, how the each of these first two lines contain poetic parallels with respect to the subject, verb, and direct object of the sentence, and a fourth component in line two, which is commonly called a *ballast variant*:

- "My soul," the subject of line one, is paralleled with "My spirit" in line two; and,

- The verb "praises" in line one is paralleled with "exults" in line two; and,

- The phrase "the greatness of the Lord" in line one is paralleled with "in God" in line two; and,

- The ballast variant "my Savior" appears only in line two.

This literary structure is common to Hebrew Scripture poetry, as even a casual reading of the Psalms by the reader will demonstrate. To sum up, Mary's obvious familiarity with the book of Psalms in the Hebrew Scriptures is quite remarkable, given that she was only about 13 years of age at the time she met Elizabeth! In perhaps a parallel to how the book of Daniel's recitation of repentant King Nebuchadnezzar's public proclamation about the grace and magnificence of God shows the clear influence of the Hebrew prophet Daniel's tutorage of the King over the years, so also does Mary's prophetic utterance reflect the influence of the Word of God to her over her short lifetime.

MARY RECITES THE WORK OF GOD

The remaining section of Mary's prophetic poem of praise recites the reason for Mary's joy at the greatness of God. Luke records her in Luke 1:48-55 as she delineates the list:

> *48 because he has looked favorably on his humble servant.*
> *From now on, all generations will call me blessed,*
> *49 because the Almighty has done great things for me.*
> *His name is holy.*

Notice, if you would please, how Mary begins her praise by expressing her view of what God has done for her personally:

- *First*, she claims that God has looked favorably toward her as his servant.

By referring to herself as the servant of God, she acknowledges her place as standing in the long tradition of the rare few who give unqualified obedience to God's call and acquiescence to his plans for her life. She also acknowledges that her servanthood is about to become recognized publicly by future generations.

- *Second*, Mary claims that God has done many great things on her behalf.

Mary also claims that the reason why God has chosen to act on her behalf is because it is in his nature to do so: he says that his "name is holy." The remainder of Mary's prophetic hymn of praise consists of Mary's list of specific ways in which God has acted, showing himself to be holy, not only on her behalf, but on behalf of God's people. Luke records the remainder of *The Magnificat* by Mary in Luke 1:50-51a with the following introductory generalization:

> *⁵⁰His mercy lasts from generation to generation for those who fear him.*
> *⁵¹He displayed his mighty power with his arm.*

Mary's statement is, of course, a direct allusion to God's own description of his nature and character as set forth in Exodus 15:5b-6 where he introduces national Israel to the Ten Commandments:

> *⁵ᵇI, the Lord your God, am a jealous God, punishing the children for the iniquity of the parents to the third and fourth generations of those who hate me, ⁶but showing gracious love to the thousandth generation of those who love me and keep my commandments.*

The next several verses of Mary's poetic utterance set forth the specific actions by which God's power has been demonstrated. Luke 1:51-55 sets forth her list of God's actions:

> *⁵¹ᵇHe scattered people who were proud in mind and heart.*

THE CHIASTIC STRUCTURE OF BIBLICAL PROPHECY

This general statement is illustrated with four specific actions. Note the chiastic order of the pronouncement, in which an A:B=B:A structure describes those who are powerful in the first line of stanza number one and the weak in the second line, and then switches the order in stanza number two to list the poor first and the rich second. Luke 1:52-53 illustrates this chiastic order:

> *⁵²He pulled powerful rulers from their thrones and lifted up humble people.*
> *⁵³He filled hungry people with good things and sent rich people away with nothing.*

This chiastic (i.e., X-like) literary structure is a common device used by Biblical writers. Perhaps the most striking use of the method of writing can be discerned by reading chapters 2-7 of the book of Daniel, where a *double chiastic structure* (i.e., A:B:C=C.B.A.) extends as far as *the subject matter* of those six chapters:

- Chapter two of the book of Daniel deals with the prophetic history of the world (as revealed to Nebuchadnezzar in his dream).

- Chapter three of the book deals with the persecution of Daniel's three friends in the famous incident of the fire furnace.

- Chapter four deals with Nebuchadnezzar's testimony about what happened when he was disciplined by God.

- Chapter five deals with the judgment of God on the unrepentant grandson of Nebuchadnezzar, which occurred the very night that Babylon fell to the Medes and the Persians.

- Chapter six deals with Daniel's own persecution, when he spent a night in the lion's den.

- Chapter seven concludes the double chiastic structure with an outline of prophetic history to come.

Notice how Mary links God's present actions, which from her personal viewpoint await their culmination in *the future*, with her parallel view suggesting that from God's standpoint, what seems to be a future event for her is an already accomplished *past tense fact*. We invite you to pay special attention to *the past tense main verb* "He helped" in Luke 1:54-55:

54He helped his servant Israel,
remembering to be merciful,
55according to the promise he made to our ancestors—
to Abraham and his descendants forever."

Two aspects of his help can be noted here: *first,* that God's activities are motivated by mercy, and *second,* that his activities on behalf of his chosen people is described in terms of God's *eternal promise* that was first articulated to Abraham and is now being ratified by the Incarnation of God's own son.

TEST #2:
ARE YOU WILLING TO GIVE
GOD YOUR EXPECTATIONS
ABOUT YOUR LIFE?

L et's review what we've learned so far about Mary, the mother of the Messiah. Her first spiritual challenge that she faced in her young life was to respond affirmatively to the question, "Are you willing to trust God with your whole life?" As we noted in the previous chapter, Mary responded to the call of God on her life by submitting to that call.

Now let's move forward in our study from the time of the Annunciation by the space of nine months. It's evident from the New Testament narrative that Mary conceived immediately upon her having said "Yes" to God's call to trust him with her whole life. However, recall, if you would please, that the key element contained in the angelic announcement to Mary at the Annunciation is this specific promise recorded in Luke 3:32-33:

...the Lord God will give him the throne of his ancestor David. ³³He will rule over the house of Jacob forever, and his kingdom will never end.

Looking back on the events from our historical perspective of 2,000 years of world history, I cannot help wondering if Mary understood precisely what was going to be involved in her saying "Yes" to cooperating with God in the birth of the Messiah. In looking at the narrative contained in Luke 2:1-20, I see four specific expectations concerning her life that Mary was being asked to surrender to God as part of his plan to make her the mother of the Messiah.

1. THE EXPECTATION ABOUT WHEN HE FULFILLS HIS PROMISES (LUKE 2:1-6)

Let's pause for a minute and think through the implications of what actually happened as the events would eventually turn out:

- The angel said *nothing* about Mary's son Jesus being rejected by Israel's leaders.

- The angel said *nothing* about him being crucified and dying a criminal's death.

- The angel said *nothing* about the time gap that would occur from the date of Messiah's birth until the start of his world reign from Jerusalem.

- The angel said *nothing* about the trauma Mary would face as a yet-unwed woman engaged to a godly Jew who had every right to divorce her on the grounds of pre-marital adultery.

- The angel said nothing about the insults that her son Jesus would bear throughout his life as a result of the gossiping that would occur as his parental heritage would be questioned. [1]

- The angel said nothing about how he would rise from the dead on the third day.

Make no mistake: each of these eventualities were mentioned in the Old Testament prophetic narratives about the rejection of Messiah. In fact, David's prophetic Psalm 22 was actually *quoted* by Jesus twice as he hung on Calvary's cross. So it's not like Mary wouldn't have been unfamiliar with the prophecies contained in the *Tanakh* about how Messiah would first be rejected, and then exalted.

Notice that if Mary expected that life was going to lead from the angelic announcement directly into the reign of Messiah, sooner or later she would learn that she needed to rethink her expectations. Frankly, things didn't turn out quite like she imagined life was going to go. Let's look forward to the ending weeks of her pregnancy and learn what happened, as recorded in Luke 2:1-20. Our first observation regarding Mary's second spiritual test is that Mary had to surrender to God her expectations regarding *when* God would fulfill his promises is described in Luke 2:1-4:

> *[1]Now in those days an order was published by Caesar Augustus that the whole world should be registered. [2]This was the first registration taken while Quirinius was governor of Syria. [3]So all the people went to their hometowns to be registered.*
> *[4]Joseph, too, went up from the city of Nazareth in Galilee to Judea, to the City of David (called Bethlehem), because he was a descendant of the household and family of David.*

---

1   See John 8:41, which contains the retort "We're not illegitimate children..." and which therefore contains the unspoken accusation by the Jewish leaders, "...like you are!" Even to the present day, the Jewish *Talmud* continues to transmit the profane tradition that Jesus, who is often referred to in that work by the anonymous moniker "So-and-So" was a *mamzer*, a Hebrew term that means an illegitimate child born out of wedlock from a fornicating wife's illicit sexual encounter with someone other than her marriage partner. For a fuller discussion of this blasphemous view, see Bruce Chilton's *The Mamzer Jesus and His Birth* cited at http://www.bibleinterp.com/articles/Chilton_Mamzer_Jesus_Birth.shtml. Chilton summaries this view by saying, "What emerges from both Rabbinic literature (supplemented by Origen) and the New Testament is that Jesus' mother was clearly known and that the identity of his father was contested."

Nothing is too difficult for God. Joseph and his betrothed wife Mary lived in Nazareth to the north of Jerusalem in Galilee, away from Bethlehem where the predicted the Messiah would be born. [2] Given that Mary was several months pregnant, and not inclined to leave the comparative safety of her family's household, it's not hard to imagine the reluctance with which she viewed any kind of travel from one city or region of Israel to another.

But God had other plans. He decided to inconvenience the whole world (including Mary and Joseph!) and therefore he put it into the mind of Rome's despotic emperor Caesar Augustus to enroll the entire Roman Empire just so his administration could finance its agenda of world-wide expansion. In order to do that, he also ordered every household to participate in a general tax-raising census. Participating in the census meant that Joseph would have to go to a family reunion of sorts by returning to his household's roots in Bethlehem:

> *⁵He went there to be registered with Mary, who had been promised to him in marriage and was pregnant. ⁶While they were there, the time came for her to have her baby,*

These verses quoted above suggest that Joseph's relationship with Mary had been an arranged betrothal. Notice the passive verb describing Mary as having "been promised to him in marriage." The identity of the persons who did the promising of her to him isn't made clear, but since we know the cultural practices of first century Israel, we can be confident that the people who did the promising were Mary's parents, working an arrangement with Joseph's parents to sustain the marital agreement.

2. THE EXPECTATION ABOUT *HOW* HE FULFILLS HIS PROMISES (LUKE 2:7)

The next observation we bring to Luke's narrative that presents us with Mary's second spiritual test is that Mary was not only being

---

2   Today, the city is also known as En Nasira, Japhia, Mash-had, en-Nasirah, Nazerat, Nazareth of Galilee, Nazareth in Galilee, and Yafti en Nasra.

tested regarding her willingness to surrender her expectations to God about *when* he was going to fulfill his plans for Mary's life, she was being asked to surrender her expectations regarding *how* he will fulfill those promises. Notice the appalling lack of kingly formality that surrounded the birth of God incarnate as Luke writes:

> *⁷and she gave birth to her first child, a son. She wrapped him in strips of cloth and laid him in a feeding trough, because there was no place for them in the guest quarters.*

Correcting a Few "Myth-conceptions" about the Birth of Jesus

The Manger Scene

There's no mention in the birth narrative of livestock being present in the stable. In fact, there's no evidence there even *was* a stable, because only a manger is mentioned by the New Testament writer. It was probably a public livestock feeding device provided as a courtesy to local ranchers. Remember the watering troughs that stood in front of saloons in the Old West here in the United States? You see them all the time in westerns. If you think that the baby Jesus was laid in the first century equivalent of a public feeding trough, the mental image you'll get won't be far off track.

Most likely, the make-shift manger had been carved out of stone, not wood. Archeological artifacts known to date from Herod's time show that the manger would have been a large single piece of stone with a carved depression in the top surface. The owner of the manger would place straw or other animal feed in the depression carved out of the stone.

Since straw makes a very unsanitary bed for a newborn, it is highly likely that Mary would have used parts of her own clothing to make a make-shift crib for Jesus. And that means she would have had to sacrifice her own clothes to do it. That's why the baby was wrapped in strips of cloth. The strips came from her own robes.

The "swaddling clothes," as the quaint King James Version of the Gospel narratives puts it, would have to have been torn from Mary's clothing by Mary herself in a make-shift first aid attempt.

She didn't have a mid-wife or relatives present to help her during her labor. In fact, the New Testament doesn't even record that Joseph was present during the birth.

The historical record does say, however, that *Mary* brought forth her first born son, that *Mary* wrapped him in strips of cloth, and that *Mary* laid him in the manger. See Luke 2:7. What Joseph was doing during this time is anybody's guess, because one other interesting fact about Joseph we learn from the New Testament is that nowhere is there ever recorded a spoken saying from him. He's never quoted as having even one word to say! In fact, he disappears completely from the life of Jesus and Mary after the Messiah's twelfth year.

There's no mention of oxen. The New Testament doesn't mention that Mary rode a donkey to Bethlehem during her pregnancy, so you can remove the donkey from the nativity scene, also. The manger wasn't necessarily made of wood. The stable (if there was one, which I doubt there was, since the Greek word for "stable" doesn't occur in the historical narrative) wouldn't have been made of wood either.

Some Thoughts on Joseph

As we noted earlier, if Joseph had been the natural father of Jesus, Jesus would have had no legal right to sit on the throne of David. My suspicion is that Joseph died while Jesus was still a teenager, making Mary a single parent when she was about thirty years old. We'll have a bit more to say about this subject when we examine Test #6: How Will You Bear the Loss of Your Spouse? starting on page 115.

We suggest that Mary never remarried, remaining a widow the rest of her life. It's possible that one of the reasons Jesus waited until the age of thirty to begin his ministry was because he was waiting for the youngest of Mary's children to grow up and move out on his own. Just before his death, Jesus turned over personal responsibility for his mother's welfare to his good friend John.

Was Mary a Working Mother after Joseph Died?

I suspect that Mary remained a working mother after Joseph died, and this time of employment continued throughout the time of Jesus' ministry, since it's highly probable that she was the person in charge of catering the wedding at Cana that you can read about in the second chapter of John's Gospel. I believe that it's highly possible that she had moved up in work status from being an indentured servant girl to running her own first-century equivalent of the catering business. That she turned to Jesus for help during the wedding party can be explained by assuming that she was in charge of the event's festivities and party supplies. Frankly, I suspect that her careful calculations over the food and drink needs of the wedding party guests would have been thrown into chaos when Jesus and twelve or more of his followers had unexpectedly appeared at the wedding feast and consumed enough of the celebration reserves to require some kind of last minute emergency remediation of the problem. I don't think Mary was expecting Jesus to perform the miracle that the New Testament records, though. His provision of a miraculous solution turned out to be the first miracle that he performed, and I think she was caught by surprise at his unexpected solution to the dilemma.

The Livestock

The livestock, if there were any, were sheep. There's no mention of livestock in the Christmas story, except for sheep, and at that time of year they were out in the fields being watched by the shepherds. That's because it was in the early spring that Jesus was born, not in the last weeks of December like we celebrate today. Here's how we know: the annunciation from the angel Gabriel to Mary took place in the sixth month of the year (Luke 1:26), i.e., in June of the Roman calendar that is still in use the world over even to this day.

The fact that this date also happened to coincide with the sixth month of Mary's cousin Elizabeth's pregnancy (Luke 1:36) has made people confuse the sixth month of the year with the sixth month of Elizabeth's pregnancy. The truth is that Elizabeth conceived in January. By adding a nine-month gestation period to the June annunciation date, you come up with sometime during the month of March or April of the next year. My guess is that the birth of Jesus the Messiah probably took place around Passover.

The traditional Christmas artwork showing Mary riding on a donkey in the direction of Bethlehem from Nazareth is not supported from the text of the New Testament birth narratives of Jesus. She is usually depicted this way because she was pregnant at the time of her and Joseph's trip to David's hometown. Artists therefore have historically *assumed* that Mary didn't walk the long distance, but the text doesn't affirm this. Nobody knows whether or not she rode a donkey. Personally, I'm of the opinion that she walked the entire distance, without aid of supplemental transportation such as a donkey.

WHY THERE WAS NO ROOM AT THE "INN"

A mid-spring birth for the Messiah about the time of the Passover would explain why the shepherds were so busy in the fields: the sheep they were tending would be sacrificed during the coming Passover celebration. With several million people crowding Jerusalem during this annual event, any possible lodging would already have been filled up by the time Mary and Joseph arrived in Bethlehem. That's one reason why they had no choice but to take lodging in a stable, nearby cave, or at least near a public manger if there wasn't a stable.

The only reason Mary and Joseph would have gone to Bethlehem during Mary's ninth month of pregnancy would be because the Romans forced them to do so. The bottom line of the trip to Bethlehem is that God used the whim of Augustus Caesar to inconvenience the entire world with an international census of both men and women in order to get Mary and Joseph to make the trip from Nazareth to Bethlehem in order to fulfill Micah's prophecy.

Here's another reason why Mary and Joseph couldn't find lodging: That Mary and Joseph, even though they were of the lineage of David, had no living relatives in Bethlehem who could offer a place to stay during Mary's labor speaks volumes about the decimation that had come to David's line since the Exile.

As noted earlier, Jeremiah 22:24-30 records a divine curse on David's lineage through Solomon to Jehoiachin (who was also known as Jeconiah): no one from David's lineage through Solomon would ever sit on the throne of Israel as King again after the Exile to Babylon. (See especially Jeremiah 22:30). Mary's husband Joseph was a part of this cursed lineage (Matthew 1:6, 11). That's why the New Testament claims that Joseph was not the father of Jesus. If he had been, Jesus would have had no legal right to sit on the throne of David. But Mary was of the lineage of David through David's son Nathan, not Solomon (Luke 3:31). Therefore as a matter of law, Mary's son Jesus had a perfect right to the throne to rule as King over Israel because that side of David's lineage had not been cursed. At any rate, over the ensuing centuries since the Exile to Babylon, so few members of David's lineage survived that no relatives remained who could exercise the Middle Eastern custom of hospitality to two distant family members visiting from the town of Nazareth, ninety miles to the north.

Frankly, the fact that two people distantly related to David could have met in Israel at all—and even then in a town ninety miles away from Bethlehem up in the northern Galilean region of Nazareth—is itself a testimony to the miraculous power of God to bring Mary and Joseph together in the first place.

3. THE EXPECTATION ABOUT *WHY* HE FULFILLS HIS PROMISES (LUKE 2:8-14)

The third observation we bring to Luke's narrative is this: Mary was not only being tested regarding her willingness to surrender her expectations to God about *when* and *how* he will fulfill those promises, she was being tested regarding her willingness to surrender to him *why* he fulfills his promises the way he does. Notice the surprising humility in which the last group of people you'd expect are presented with an angelic press conference on the evening of the birth of Jesus the Messiah. Luke writes:

> *[8]In that region there were shepherds living in the fields, watching their flock during the night. [9]An angel of the Lord*

> *appeared to them, and the glory of the Lord shone around*
> *them, and they were terrified. [10] Then the angel told them,*
> *"Stop being afraid! Listen! I am bringing you good news of*
> *great joy for all the people. [11] Today your Savior, the Lord*
> *Messiah, was born in the City of David. [12] And this will be a*
> *sign for you: You will find a baby wrapped in strips of cloth*
> *and lying in a feeding trough."*

This event shows us that Mary was learning that the Messiah's birth (and even news about his actual identity as the rightful successor to King David) won't necessarily be given to the beautiful, aristocratic people of Israel. No, after revealing himself to Mary, he chose a bunch of shepherds to whom the news is to come.

God makes his most profound announcements to the most unusual people. He doesn't necessarily choose the wealthy, the powerful, or those born of nobility to demonstrate his greatness or to show his power. Usually, the only wealthy, powerful, or noble born people who learn what the power of God is all about are the ones who are about to be disciplined by him, and even then that discipline is likely to be fatal. The Pharaoh of Egypt who ruled that nation at the time of the exodus of Israel is an example of this, as was Babylonian King Nebuchadnezzar's grandson, who saw the fingers of a man's hand write out his judgment decree on the wall of his palace. You can read that story in the fifth chapter of the book of Daniel.

So we're faced with the questions, "Why did God reveal his promise the way the Gospel of Luke records the story in Luke 2:8-14? Why didn't he send Gabriel to announce the imminent birth to Herod and to the intelligentsia of his regime? If Gabriel had done so, couldn't he have given Herod a warning not to mess with Mary, Joseph, and the baby Jesus, just as God had warned Abraham's oppressor not to mess with the man's wife Sarah?"

The answer to this line of inquiry is that God has not chosen the wise, powerful, or rich of this world to inherit his kingdom. The mark of God's omnipotence and worth is illustrated in how he chooses to treat those whom the world ignores as being irrelevant, useless, and of no possible use. Just as Jesus announced his own Messiahship to a socially ostracized woman one hot sunny day near a well when there was nobody there but him and a serial adulterer from whom he asked for some water, and just as he refused to discuss his true nature with Jerusalem's leaders until the very day of his trial before the Sanhedrin, so also will the angels bring their divine press conference to a bunch of shepherds and not to ancient Israel's elite:

> [13]*Suddenly, a multitude of the Heavenly Army appeared with the angel, praising God by saying,* [14]*"Glory to God in the highest, and peace on earth to people who enjoy his favor!"*

4. THE EXPECTATION ABOUT HOW HIS FULFILLMENT WILL CHANGE HER LIFE (LUKE 2:15-20)

It would appear from the rest of Luke's narrative concerning the nativity of Jesus that Mary didn't send out any birth announcements. She didn't have to, since the shepherds who came to visit did this for her. The Gospel writer records the story in Luke 2:15-20:

> [15]*When the angels had left them and gone back to heaven, the shepherds told one another, "Let's go to Bethlehem and see what has taken place that the Lord has told us about."* [16]*So they went quickly and found Mary and Joseph with the baby, who was lying in the feeding trough.* [17]*When they saw this, they repeated what they had been told about this child.* [18]*All who heard it were amazed at what the shepherds told them.* [19]*However, Mary continued to treasure all these things in her heart and to ponder them.* [20]*Then the shepherds returned to their flock, glorifying and praising God for everything they had heard and seen, just as it had been told to them.*

Do note, if you would please, that as soon as they confirmed the angelic announcement by locating the baby Jesus in the feeding trough (which, by the way, gives us a not-so-subtle hint that the location where Mary and the baby Jesus were staying was probably a very public place, open to the elements, and ***not*** inside a stable), the visiting shepherds repeated what they had been told about the child.

We're not told how many people had arrived at the birth scene by the time they arrived. Mary and the baby Jesus were present, of course. Joseph might have been there, but the text doesn't mention him by name. Of course, as we noted earlier, Joseph's presence in the nativity narrative is minimized in significance by the Gospel writers, and he's never even quoted once in the New Testament as having had anything to say of relevance to the events described. But the notation by Luke that the shepherds had an audience of considerable size is made when Luke records the response of "all who heard it," which clearly connotes the impression to the reader that a large number of people were witnesses to the shepherds' testimony regarding what they had seen when they were out in the fields that night, and that they were unanimous in their conclusion that the events described were quite remarkable.

The hint contained in this narrative that gives us a clue as to the impact this visit had on Mary is contained in Luke 2:19, where we are told that "Mary continued to treasure all these things in her heart and to ponder them." Is this a hint that it was slowly dawning on her that her expectations regarding *when, how,* and *why* God was going to fulfill his promises to her needed to be surrendered to God? We think so.

We also suspect that her quiet, judicious, introspective silence as she mulled over the events of the day in her mind was leading her to realize that all of the events were going to affect her life in a way that she could not otherwise have imagined.

TEST #3:
ARE YOU WILLING
TO WALK WITH GOD
INTO HEARTBREAK?

WHEN GOD WARNS THERE'S TROUBLE AHEAD...

R ight in the middle of the very first public address by Jesus the Messiah to his followers as the promised and rightful king of Israel, the son of Mary summarizes his counsel regarding the spiritual priorities of life by instructing his disciples in Matthew 5:33-34 as follows:

> *33...first be concerned about God's kingdom and his righteousness, and all of these things will be provided for you as well. 34So never worry about tomorrow, because tomorrow will worry about itself. Each day has enough trouble of its own.*

Nowhere is this counsel more true or applicable than when we study the life of Mary, the mother of Jesus the Messiah. The third spiritual test that Mary is appointed by God to undergo is presented to her only about forty days after her son was born in Bethlehem. In this challenge, she must answer the test question, "Are you willing to walk with God into heartbreak?" The story in which Mary faces this challenge is related to us in Luke 2:21-38, when the infant Jesus is presented in the Temple for the first time. I see four factors that come to mind as I read through Luke's narrative of the events that occurred 40 days after Jesus was born. Let's study them together....

1. Are You Willing to Suffer even though You've Been Faithful to God's Word? (Luke 2:21-24)

Our first observation about Mary's third test regarding whether or not she was willing to walk with God into heartbreak, is found in Luke's introductory comment to Luke's narrative regarding the presentation of the infant Jesus to God in keeping with the requirements of the Law. Luke writes:

>*²¹After eight days had passed, the infant was circumcised and named Jesus, the name given him by the angel before he was conceived in the womb.*

We invite the reader to note the passive verb used by Luke to describe the naming of Jesus in this verse. Jewish tradition dictated that the name of a first-born son was to be assigned by the father (no doubt with contributing desires of the mother taken into account). But in the case of Jesus' birth, Joseph is not listed as the person who gave the infant his name *Jesus*. Mary is assigned the credit for doing this, and for her part, she is merely following the instructions that had been supplied to her by the angel Gabriel. Joseph is omitted from the child's naming rights because he wasn't the biological father of Jesus.

A week after Jesus' birth, on the eighth day following that event, a 33-day long waiting period for ritual purification was completed by Mary. When the time came to complete the ritual sacrifices called for in the book of Leviticus, we read as follows what happened on the 40th day after Jesus was born. Luke writes in Luke 2:22-24:

> *22 When the time came for their purification according to the Law of Moses, Joseph and Mary took Jesus up to Jerusalem to present him to the Lord, 23 as it is written in the Law of the Lord, "Every firstborn son is to be designated as holy to the Lord." 24 They also offered a sacrifice according to what is specified in the Law of the Lord: "a pair of turtledoves or two young pigeons."*

The presentation of the infant Jesus in the Temple was, strictly speaking, done by the book; that is, Mary and Joseph followed the regulation set forth in Leviticus 12:8, the full context of which we can read in Leviticus 12:1-8:

> *1 The LORD told Moses, 2 "Tell the Israelis that a woman who conceives and bears a son is unclean for seven days. Just like the days of her menstruation, she is unclean. 3 On the eighth day, the flesh of the baby's foreskin is to be circumcised. 4 For 33 days after this, she is to remain in purification due to her blood loss. She is not to touch any sacred thing or enter the sanctuary until the days of her purification have been completed. …*
> *6 When the days of her purification have been completed, whether for her son or daughter, she is to bring to the priest at the entrance to the Tent of Meeting a one year old lamb for a whole burnt offering or a young dove for a sin offering. 7 He is to offer it in the LORD's presence and make atonement for her so that she becomes clean from her blood loss.*

ON MARY'S SACRIFICES

For those of our readers who may be inclined to hold the view that Mary was conceived without a sin nature, a doctrine that is called the *Immaculate Conception* in Catholicism, we invite you to take another look at the rationale behind Mary's sacrifice. Leviticus

12:6-7 clearly refers to one of the offerings being a sin offering for the mother in order to "make atonement for her." This requirement is explained for us *a second time* in the very next verses recorded in the book of Leviticus, the third book in the *Torah*, which read:

> *This is the law concerning the bearing of a male or female child. ⁸If she cannot afford a goat, then two turtledoves or two young doves—one for a burnt offering and the other for a sin offering—will serve for him to make atonement for her, so that she becomes clean."*

In this repetition of the requirement, we are informed that one of Mary's offerings was a *burnt offering given in thanks for the child* and the other was a *sin offering on behalf of the mother*. By complying with Leviticus 2:8's requirement to make atonement for herself, Mary is offering what God requires to satisfy her need for an atonement for her sin. Accordingly, by presenting the two offerings in the Temple on the occasion of Jesus' presentation on the 40ᵗʰ day following childbirth, Mary is confessing publicly that she has a sinful nature that needs atonement in order to satisfy the righteous requirements of God. To sum up, Mary herself repudiated the doctrine of *Immaculate Conception* by offering a sin offering for herself. If the New Testament was ever to record that she was born without a sinful nature, Luke's record of Mary's sacrifice on the 40ᵗʰ day following the birth of her son would have been the time to mention that dogma. But it doesn't.

2. ARE YOU WILLING TO SUFFER EVEN WHEN GOD CONFIRMS HIS INTENTIONS AHEAD OF TIME? (LUKE 2:25-32)

There's more to Mary's third test than just having to deal with the predicted heartbreak that will come even though she will have done everything required by God's law. Our second observation about whether Mary is willing to walk with God into heartbreak relates to her willingness to walk into that heartbreak *in the midst of a clear warning from God that those troubles were sure to come soon.*

Just as Mary and Joseph were involved in presenting Jesus and their offerings in the Temple, and by doing so were being faithful to keep standards set forth in the Word of God regarding their newly born infant, by divine appointment an elderly man named Simeon appears on the Temple grounds during a visit or pilgrimage to Jerusalem. Luke writes in Luke 2:25-32 as follows:

> *²⁵Now a man named Simeon was in Jerusalem. This man was righteous and devout. He was waiting for the one who would comfort Israel, and the Holy Spirit was upon him. ²⁶It had been revealed to him by the Holy Spirit that he would not die until he had seen the Lord's Messiah.*
> *²⁷Led by the Spirit, he went into the Temple. When the parents brought the child Jesus to do for him what was customary under the Law, ²⁸Simeon took the infant in his arms and praised God, saying,*
> *²⁹"Master, now you are dismissing your servant in peace according to your promise,*
> *³⁰because my eyes have seen your salvation,*
> *³¹which you prepared for all people to see—*
> *³²a light that will reveal salvation to unbelievers and bring glory to your people Israel."*

The arrangement and tone of what Simeon had to say to God at this moment was crafted by him spontaneously in the form of a prophetic utterance, similar in scope and majesty to the formula of an Isaiah or Jeremiah, two of the major prophets of the *Tanakh*, or Hebrew Scriptures. The statement is *poetic* in form and substance.

3. ARE YOU WILLING TO SUFFER EVEN WHEN YOUR EXPECTATIONS DON'T TURN OUT THE WAY YOU IMAGINED? (LUKE 2:33-38)

What Simeon had to say was nothing less than startling to both Mary and Joseph: Luke 2:33 tells us that "Jesus' father and mother kept wondering at the things being said about him." Let's stop for a moment and recall the divine pronouncement given to Mary nine months earlier. She had been told that her son was to inherit the throne of David, and that he would rule over the nation of Israel forever. Given what Simeon is about to say, it's not surprising that Mary and Joseph would be confused. That's because what Simon predicts is *anything* but encouraging.

SIMEON'S PREDICTION OF COMING HEARTBREAK

Without warning or other preparation, Simeon makes a dark prediction about future events that will affect Jesus and his mother. Specifically, Luke tells us:

> [34] *Then Simeon blessed them and told Mary, his mother,*
> *"This infant is destined to cause many in Israel to fall and*
> *rise. Also, he will be a sign that will be opposed.* [35] *Indeed,*
> *a sword will pierce your own soul, too, so that the inner*
> *thoughts of many people might be revealed."*

Why is Simeon telling Mary that Jesus is going to be a stumbling block for the majority of the Jews living in Israel at that time *a blessing*? We suggest that by warning Mary that "many in Israel" will fall, nevertheless there's a ray of hope in the man's pronouncement, too, because many will be uplifted. But at the same time, Simeon unmistakably warns Mary that a sword will pierce her soul. The events surrounding Messiah's life will serve as a spiritual litmus test of sorts that will reveal the motivations of many people. The clear implications of this warning is that the motivations that will be revealed will be dark and antagonistic toward the Messiah.

Note also, if you would, how Joseph's participation in the future life of Mary and Joseph is not mentioned by Simeon. Many Biblical scholars see the deliberate omission of Joseph from Simeon's prediction as a secondary, ominous warning of trouble ahead. The implication that seems to be connoted by Joseph's absence from Simeon's dark prediction is that Joseph will not live to see the shadowy days that are coming for Mary and Jesus.

ANNA: THE LITTLE OLD LADY

The written ministry of prophetic utterance is commonly considered to have ended with the work of the prophet Malachi in the mid-'400s BC. But the oral office had not died out yet by the time Mary and Joseph arrived to present Jesus in the Temple. As a point of historical certainty, the office continued well into the middle of the first century, as even a casual reading of the book of Acts will document. In the case study presented to us by Luke, Anna is described as a widow who had lived for about 84 years following the death of her husband (Luke 2:37). Given that she had been married for only seven years before her husband died, that means Anna was more than 100 years old by the time she ran into Mary, Joseph, and the infant Jesus in the Temple. Luke informs us in Luke 2:36-38:

> *[36] Now Anna, a prophetess, was also there. She was a descendant of Phanuel from the tribe of Asher. She was very old, having lived with her husband for seven years after her marriage, [37] and then as a widow for 84 years. She never left the Temple, but continued to worship there night and day with times of fasting and prayer. [38] Just then she came forward and began to thank God and to speak about Jesus to everyone who was waiting for the redemption of Jerusalem.*

The sum and substance of Mary bumping into Simeon and Anna is that when God's word required that it was time to present Jesus to the community of faith in the Temple, he revealed this momentous event to a homeless old bag lady who had no place to lay her head at night anywhere else than in an unused store room in the Temple and to an old man who happened to come along at the right time to the right place.

4. ARE YOU WILLING TO SUFFER EVEN WHEN YOUR OWN HOMETOWN REJECTS YOU? (LUKE 2:39-40)

Our fourth and final observation concerning Mary's challenge to answer affirmatively that she was willing to walk with God into heartbreak is set forth in Luke's seemingly innocuous conclusion to the incident of the presentation of Jesus in the Temple by Mary and Joseph. Luke writes in Luke 2:39-40 about where the family would be settling after their presentation of Jesus in the Temple:

> *[39] After doing everything required by the Law of the Lord, Joseph and Mary returned to their hometown of Nazareth in Galilee. [40] Meanwhile, the child continued to grow and to become strong. He was filled with wisdom, and God's favor rested upon him.*

We invite the reader to keep in mind that the infant Jesus had been born in Bethlehem 40 days antecedent to the presentation of him in the Temple by Mary and Joseph. It's virtually *impossible* for Mary and Joseph to have traveled from Bethlehem north back to Nazareth, and then back to Jerusalem in order to present the post-natal offerings required by Leviticus 2:8, to which Luke's narrative refers. There wouldn't have been enough time to make the overland journey on foot.

But there would have been plenty of time for them to have made the short walk from Bethlehem to the city of David that lay annexed on the south side of Jerusalem, where the Temple would have been located. That would have been only about 200 yards south of the Antonia Fortress complex, the remains of which are still visible to this day in the old city of Jerusalem.

Note, though, how Mary and Joseph returned to Nazareth immediately upon the conclusion of the incidents recorded in the second chapter of the Gospel of Luke. That's because Nazareth was their home town. But within two years after their return to Nazareth, Mary and Joseph were forced to return to Bethlehem. We know that the family returned to Bethlehem about two years after the Temple incident described in Luke 2 because it was to this city that the magi would travel in order to present their gifts to the infant Messiah.

We suggest that in Nazareth, Mary and Joseph would have faced continual reproach due to the constant skepticism voiced by their neighbors, who were only too aware of the claim by Mary that she had become pregnant antecedent to the completion of her marriage betrothal to Joseph. But in Bethlehem, Mary and Joseph were small-town heroes. Dozens, if not hundreds, of the local residents had heard the testimony given by the visiting shepherds who had related their tale of a visit by an army of angelic beings as they announced the birth of the Messiah.

To sum up our final observation concerning Mary's third test as to whether she was willing to walk with God into heartbreak, Mary had to face the constant criticisms, the behind-the-back whispering, and the slanderous accusations that Joseph wasn't really the father of Jesus. The constant disparagement finally took its toll on Mary and Joseph, so the family relocated to Bethlehem, just in time to receive a visit from the magi and then to leave Israel for the next several years as they waited for a signal from God to return to Israel.

Test #4:
Will You Give God
Your Illusion of
Personal Security?

The Safest Place to Be is the Center of God's Will

Have you ever found yourself in a situation in which you should have or could have been seriously injured—or even killed—but somehow you escaped? Sometimes those who place their unconditional trust in God find themselves walking right into danger as a consequence of that trust. Now with respect to the situation in which Mary the Mother of Jesus was immersed following her decision to cooperate with God in the birth of the Messiah, certain events began to unfold over which this young Jewish teenager had absolutely no control.

As a result, within a few weeks following her decision to trust God with her whole life, Mary was confronted with what we're calling the fourth spiritual test of her life: she was faced with the all-important choice as to whether or not she would be giving to God her illusion of personal security. Let's study how this came about in the story of what happened after the birth of her firstborn son Jesus. Matthew 2:1-25 discusses the crisis that she faced, and how it was resolved. In looking over this narrative, eight basic observations come to mind. Let's study them together.

1. JERUSALEM'S PUBLIC SCANDAL CREATED (MATTHEW 2:1-3)

Unknown to Mary and Joseph, an unexpected time of scandal erupted. A couple of years has passed since Jesus had been born in Bethlehem. As we noted in the previous chapter, Jesus had been presented in the Temple by his mother and father on the 40th day following his birth, and the family had returned to their home town of Nazareth following their registration for the census enumerated at the decree of Caesar Augustus. But as we noted at the end of our discussion of Mary's third test, Mary and Joseph had moved back to Bethlehem from Nazareth, in our estimation probably because of the accusations flying around Nazareth about Mary's conception of Jesus before Joseph and Mary had started living together. Two years later, however, Matthew 2:1-3 adds a few additional factors to the story of the early years of Jesus young life:

> *¹After Jesus had been born in Bethlehem of Judea during the reign of King Herod, wise men arrived in Jerusalem from the east ²and asked, "Where is the one who was born king of the Jews? We saw his star in the east and have come to worship him."*
> *³When King Herod heard this, he was disturbed, as was all of Jerusalem.*

CORRECTING SOME MORE "MYTH-CONCEPTIONS" ABOUT THE BIRTH OF JESUS

During the twenty centuries that have passed since Jesus the

Messiah was born in Bethlehem, myriads of non-historical "facts" have threaded their way into the story of the Nativity events. What the New Testament really tells about the first Christmas—as opposed to what most people commonly think it says—is amazing enough in its own right that embellishments don't need to be added years after the fact. So let's study some more of the more popular "myth-conceptions" about the "First Noel" as part of our analysis of Mary's fourth spiritual test.

Figure 16: The Magi by Henry Siddons Mowbray, 1915.

ABOUT THE WISE MEN

There weren't necessarily three of them. Nobody knows their names. One of them wasn't black. They weren't astrologers or even astronomers, for that matter. They never joined the shepherds in worshiping the Messiah as a baby. They never visited Bethlehem during the time Mary and Joseph were in the stable, if there even was a stable, since it's highly probable that Mary, Joseph, and the baby Jesus never even lodged in one while they were in Bethlehem. The Los Angeles Griffith Observatory may be right when it claims that a rare conjunction of planets which occurred about 5 BC was visible from the Middle East—but that has nothing to do with the Christmas story.

Figure 17: The Magi by Armand Seranno

The conjunction wasn't the "star" that guided the Wise Men to Bethlehem. In fact, the star never guided the Wise Men to Bethlehem at all. If that star led them anywhere from the East, it led them to Jerusalem and to Herod, not to Bethlehem and to the baby Jesus.

Here's what we do know about the Wise Men: They were probably godly Jewish believers who had remained in the region of Babylon or perhaps Susa after the collapse of the Babylonian and Medo-Persian empires. Having made their homeland in the economically rich Fertile Crescent area far to the north and east of Jerusalem, some of these Jews rose to high prominence in the ranks of the political empires of their day.

The Old Testament tells the stories of eight such men and one woman, all of whom played significant roles in the political arenas of Babylon and Medo-Persia during the Jewish Exile and afterwards. These individuals include Shadrach, Meshach, Abed-nego, and the prophet Daniel, all of whom are mentioned in the Book of Daniel. The story of Nehemiah appears in the book that bears his name for its title, as does Ezra in the book named after him. Queen Esther and Mordecai are the focus of the Book of Esther. Daniel and his three friends are given the occupational title "Magi" by the Book of Daniel, which means that the Magi of the New Testament most likely would have been political consultants to powerful rulers of the first century, BC.

Making their hometown as far to the North and East as they would have, the Wise Men couldn't have been guided to Jerusalem— or even to Bethlehem—by a star that was only visible in the East. That's because Jerusalem and Bethlehem lay to the West and South of their homeland. If it had gone before them as a guiding light, the star would have had to travel ahead of them, first to the North, then to the West, and finally to the South as the entourage traced its way over the Fertile Crescent from the Tigris-Euphrates area to Palestine.

THE VISIT TO BETHLEHEM

As we above, nobody knows how many wise men there were. The Christmas "myth-conception" of three Wise Men comes from the three types of gifts offered to Mary and Joseph: gold, frankincense, and myrrh. However, there could not have been only three Magi who dropped in to visit Herod because a visit by only three foreign king makers wouldn't have caused the public scandal described in Matthew 2:3.

It is more than likely that there would have been about a hundred or more people in the complete entourage, if you count the security forces that would have accompanied the Magi to protect them from highway robbers that were known to frequent the main trade routes from the Far East. The phenomenal wealth given to Mary and Joseph also would have needed guarding along the way. Since the gold that was given to Jesus' parents would later prove to be sufficient to fund their extended sojourn in Egypt, it is extremely likely that these funds would have been guarded by a large force.

If you count the preparation time needed to mount an expedition of one or two hundred people from Medo-Persia to Palestine, the total journey to visit the child probably took about two years—at least that's how long the Magi told Herod it had been since they had seen the star in their homeland in the East. By the time the Magi arrived in Palestine, baby Jesus would have been nearly two years old—and long gone from the manger in Bethlehem.

That's one reason why the Magi didn't bother to travel directly to Bethlehem to visit the child upon their arrival in the greater Jerusalem area. They logically figured—but all too *inaccurately*, it turned out—that Jesus and his parents had left Bethlehem during the previous two years. As a result, it probably came as a surprise to them when the star finally did guide them to Bethlehem after all. If the Magi had followed the intelligence information already in their possession, they never would have run into Herod and his cronies. And there never would have been a Bethlehem massacre. See what happens when you aren't faithful to follow up on the information you already have?

The detail about the manger demonstrates that the Magi visited Bethlehem much later than the first Christmas night. Jesus was placed in a manger after his birth (Luke 2:7). But the Magi visited Him in a house (Matthew 2:11).

The text of the New Testament never *quite* gets around to claiming The Messiah was born in a stable. As we pointed out earlier, the *Holy Bible: International Standard Version* translates the Greek term **καταλύματι** (katalúmati) as "guest quarters." Luke 2:7 only says the baby Jesus was laid in a feeding trough by his mother. The text never really says that the feeding trough was located inside a stable. (I'll have more to say about the scene, below.)

The Magi never asked where the child had been born. But they did want to know where he was two years after his birth. They already knew that he had been born in Bethlehem, since they would have been familiar with the prophecies of Micah 5:2.

But Herod wasn't informed about the Biblical prophecy. That's why it was *Herod* who did the asking (Matthew 2:3-4). His intelligence team came up with the right answer—much to the dismay of the Bethlehem inhabitants, who suffered the loss of about thirty or forty baby boys from the age of birth to two years old when Herod ordered the massacre of the children.

Another reason we know the Magi didn't visit Bethlehem the night of the birth was that Mary and Joseph only offered a pair of turtle doves as a birth offering (Luke 2:24) following her ritual purification after childbirth. As we've already observed, this purification rite took place 40 days after the birth of Jesus. To offer a pair of turtle doves was the least expensive offering allowed under the Old Testament regulations.

If the Magi had appeared the night of the birth of The Messiah, Mary and Joseph would have had enough money to present a more expensive offering. Also, since the historical record indicates that Mary, Joseph, and the baby Jesus left for Egypt the very night the Magi visited them (Matthew 2:12-13), there wouldn't have been enough time to wait for the eighth day of Jesus' life in order to circumcise him (Luke 2:21), let alone wait through the several weeks needed until the post-natal purification rite could be performed.

WHAT ABOUT THE "STAR"?

The "star" that preceded the Magi wasn't a constellation or conjunction of planets. The Gospel writer Luke was an intelligent man—an educated physician, in fact. He knew the difference between a phenomenon that is visible in interplanetary or interstellar space and a phenomenon that is visible in the atmosphere above the earth.

For one thing, the text of the New Testament clearly says that the star moved with respect to the observers (Matthew 2:9). Stars and their conjunctions, as any rational observer notes, do not so move. They appear to be rigidly fixed as lights in the firmament. In fact, they are so rigidly fixed that the oceans can be navigated by them.

Furthermore, the Greek word for "interplanetary conjunction" or "constellation" is not used by Luke to describe the star (the Greek word *astērion*). Dr. Luke uses the regular Greek word **ἀστήρ** (*astēr*), instead. The most likely explanation for the "star" phenomenon can be found by looking at its Old Testament parallel, the Shekinah cloud of fire that accompanied the children of Israel out of Egypt. The glory of God in visible form traveled in front of the Israelites, giving guidance and protection during their Exodus wanderings.

We suggest that the phenomenon referred to by the Magi was a temporary re-appearance of this same visible glory of God. It appeared to them while they were back home in Medo-Persia, instructing them to make their journey to Israel. When they finally arrived in Palestine, the Shekinah reappeared

Figure 18: Woodcut of Herod the Great.
Source: https://en.wikipedia.org/wiki/Herod_the_Great

91

as a visible guide to help them find the home where Mary, Joseph, and Jesus were residing.

BETHLEHEM VS. NAZARETH

We've already noted that Mary and Joseph didn't stay in Bethlehem by first choice. Following the birth of Jesus, they tried to go back to Nazareth at first (Luke 2:39). Within two years they were back at Bethlehem living in a house where they would eventually meet the Magi (Matthew 2:11).

I think the reason they went back to Nazareth from Bethlehem was they didn't have any relatives who lived in Bethlehem. They had no family roots. All their friends lived in Nazareth.

Figure 19: Modern aerial view of Masada, in the Judaean Desert. Note the Dead Sea in the distance.
Image source: https://upload.wikimedia.org/wikipedia/commons/1/14/Israel-2013-Aerial_21-Masada.jpg

Figure 20: Modern ruins of Herodium, approximately 7.5 miles south of Jerusalem.
Image source: https://upload.wikimedia. org/wikipedia/commons/5/5f/-Herodium_ from_above_2.jpg

Figure 21: Modern day ruins of Caesarea Maritima.
https://upload.wikimedia.org/wikipedia/ commons/¬b/bb/-Caesarea_maritima_% 28DerHexer%29_2011-08-02_098.jpg

That's why they returned home to Nazareth following Jesus' circumcision and Mary's ritual purification. But they didn't stay there. I suspect it's because of the scandal of Mary's pregnancy out of wedlock with what appeared to be Joseph's child. Mary and Joseph would have been social outcasts.

Luke records that the popular myth that Joseph was the father of Jesus persisted at least through the time when he wrote the Gospel of Luke (Luke 3:23); i.e., the middle of the first century, AD. In fact, during the Messiah's lifetime, the Pharisees employed a personal attack against Jesus based on a challenge to the legitimacy of His birth. This happened on at least one occasion (John 8:41). It had doubtlessly been noised about that at one time Joseph had thought about beginning divorce proceedings against Mary, but had changed his mind.

At any rate, things would have been very uncomfortable for Jesus, Mary, and Joseph had they stayed in Nazareth. But Bethlehem was a different story. They may have been social outcasts in Nazareth, but in Bethlehem they were small-town heroes. The story of the shepherd's vision of angels doubtlessly had been spread all over the little village. The prophetic messages from Simeon (Luke 2:25-35) and Anna (Luke 2:36-37) about the great things in store for Jesus had been told to all who would listen (Luke 2:38). I think Jesus and His family moved back to Bethlehem to escape Nazareth gossip.

And God used Mary and Joseph's reaction to the Nazareth scandal as the means to guide them back to Bethlehem in time to meet the Magi so they could receive the funding needed to keep them alive during their Egyptian sojourn. You might keep that in mind next time you're tempted to think God doesn't provide during adversity. God never abandoned His Son, and he is just as faithful today to anyone who will put their trust in him.

2. God's Prophecy Fulfilled (Matthew 2:4-7)

All of the troubles through which God's people travel are Father-filtered. Nothing occurs by happenstance, and every event is part of his greater plan for us and for his agenda in the world. In the case of Mary and Joseph's temporary living quarters in Bethlehem, God's sovereign appointment of the timing of the visit by the Magi demonstrates that God can even use the *mistaken behavior* of his emissaries to accomplish his will. Notice, if you would, how the writer speaks of their visit in the second chapter of Matthew's Gospel:

> *[4]He called together all the high priests and scribes of the people and asked them where the Messiah was to be born.*
> *[5]They told him, "In Bethlehem of Judea, because that is what was written by the prophet:*
> *[6]'O Bethlehem in the land of Judah,*
> *you are by no means least among the rulers of Judah,*
> *because from you will come a ruler*
> *who will shepherd my people Israel.'"*
> *[7]Then Herod secretly called together the wise men, found out from them the time the star had appeared, [8]and sent them to Bethlehem.*

That rascal Herod was a cunning strategic planner when it comes to securing his hold on his governorship of the land of first century Israel, vassal though he was of Rome. The man held a dubious reputation among the Jews of Mary's day. Considered by political conservatives as only a subservient client king appointed by Rome, he has been described as an insane governor who murdered his own family, along with a large number of rabbis, in order to maintain his secure hold on the throne of Israel.[1] The *Jewish Encyclopedia* claims that he "was prepared to commit any crime in order to gratify his unbounded ambition."[2] Conversely, Herod was respected because he was also known for his colossal building projects throughout Judea, including his expansion of the Second Temple in Jerusalem, the construction of the Mediterranean port at Caesarea Maritima, and the fortresses at Masada and Herodium.

---

1   Spino, Ken (Rabbi) (2010). "History Crash Course #31: Herod the Great (online)." *Crash Course in Jewish History*. Targum Press. ISBN 978-1-5687-1532-2. *Retrieved 7 May 2013.*

2   For further reading, see http://jewishencyclopedia.com/articles/7598-herod-i.

3. HEROD'S DECEPTION INITIATED (MATTHEW 2:8)

The commencement of what will swiftly become Herod's *pogrom* to annihilate any possible nascent threat to his regime begins with an outwardly innocent statement by him to the visiting Magi. Notice how Matthew 2:8 records Herod's succinct set of instructions to the visiting delegation from the ancient city of Babylon. (It's possible that they might have come from Susa):

> *8He told them, "As you go, search carefully for the child. When you find him, tell me so that I, too, may go and worship him."*

Don't believe for a minute that Herod had any intentions of worshipping the infant Jesus as God incarnate. The man was a pagan Roman. If he had any belief that one of the members of his Roman pantheon of gods could become man, he wasn't the type of despotic ruler to admit it to a retinue of visiting king makers from Babylon. Furthermore, the man's worldview would have been a million miles distant from the Hebrew concept of the infinitely perfect Creator of heaven and earth clothing himself in human form consistent with Biblical prophecy. If he worshipped any human being, he worshipped himself. His statement to the visiting dignitaries was intended for their private consumption only, and as the events quickly unfolded, Herod's pronouncement would prove itself to be nothing less than a bald-faced lie.

4. THE MAGI'S PILGRIMAGE COMPLETED (MATTHEW 2:9-12)

Notice, if you would please, how Matthew's narrative informs us that the Magi listened respectfully to King Herod and then proceeded to follow the intelligence information they had *already* received from the Shekinah glory of God that had guided them from their homeland to the Jerusalem area. Matthew 2:9-12 informs us:

> *9After listening to the king, they set out, and the star they had seen in the east went ahead of them until it came and stopped over the place where the child was. 10When they saw the star, they were ecstatic with joy. 11After they went into the house and saw the child with his mother Mary, they fell down and*

worshipped him. Then they opened their treasure sacks and
offered him gifts of gold, frankincense, and myrrh.
[12]Having been warned in a dream not to go back to Herod,
they left for their own country by a different road.

We invite the reader to note, if you would please, the reaction
of the Magi upon seeing Jesus and Mary: they fell to the ground
and worshipped him. Given that these Magi were most likely Jewish
king makers; that is, aristocratic members of the ruling class that still
held sway in the remnants of the Medo-Persian empire that once
ruled large areas of the Middle East, it would not be considered
appropriate to bow down to a human being after the manner in
which their ancestor Abraham bowed down to worship the Living
God. But these people were doing *precisely that* to a two-year-old
child. We conclude from this narrative that even at an early age of
about two years old, it was evident to those who looked closely that
Jesus of Nazareth, human child though he was, was also a hybrid
being – 100% human being and 100% deity.

ABOUT THOSE GIFTS

We won't dwell for long on the nature of the gifts presented
by the magi to the infant Jesus, except to remind our readers that
the tradition that there were three Magi who visited Mary, Joseph,
and their young child Jesus came from the three different types of
gifts presented. The more likely scenarios is that there could have
been dozens of people in the complete entourage, not counting any
security forces that accompanied them in the long, arduous journey
that would have started in Babylonia and led them north, west,
and then south as they traversed the Fertile Crescent area of the
Levant on their way to Bethlehem.

But then again, the three gifts each had distinct and separate
purposes for having been given to Mary and Joseph, to be held in
trust by them for use by Jesus in his childhood and adulthood:

- The gold would have been used to finance their coming trip
  to Egypt, though at the time of its presentation into the care

and custody of Jesus' parents, neither the Magi nor Joseph and Mary could have foreseen that this wealth would be needed to finance their extended exile in Egypt.

- The myrrh was a fragrant spice, commonly (though not always) used to anoint a body after death in anticipation of burial. If your reaction to learning this fact is one of surprise, you can imagine how Mary must have felt. After all, how would *you* react if as you were raising your first-born son, one day when he was about two years old a diplomat from a faraway country came to visit *you* at your own home, replete with a full entourage and security detail? Imagine further how you might react if this ambassador were to present as a gift to your child a bottle of formaldehyde, which is today's equivalent of myrrh. Wouldn't you conclude from this gift being presented by the ambassador that at one point in the future, your son is going to die, and that he probably will die before you do? Come to think of it, when she thought about the gift of myrrh, Mary might have been tempted to conclude that the gold was intended to finance her son's coming funeral, since she didn't know she'd be leaving for Egypt until later that evening.

Figure 22: The Massacre of the Innocents at Bethlehem by Matteo di Giovanni. Note the portrayal utilizing the sartorial style of the mid-15th century Renaissance. Image source: https://upload.wikimedia. org/wikipedia/commons/1/1b/Matteo_di_ Giovanni_002.jpg

- Perhaps Mary might have thought that the frankincense, which was traditionally burned as part of Jewish prayers, was also intended to be used during her coming time of mourning.

Today, looking at the gifts presented by the Magi through the lens of 2,000 years of history, perhaps it's way too easy to remove their presentations and offerings from the realm of the practical to the realm of the symbolic and spiritual. I'm not persuaded that Mary would have interpreted the three types of gifts as anything less than *harbingers of death.*

To sum up, I think Mary considered these gifts to be warnings that hazardous times were on the horizon. She didn't know it with certainty, but those hazardous times began almost immediately. Notice how Matthew 2:13-15 informs us what happened after the magi had left Bethlehem, later that same night:

5. JESUS' PROTECTION ENSURED (MATTHEW 2:13-15)

Our analysis of the events surrounding Mary's fourth spiritual test question, "Will you give to God your illusion of personal security?" comes to its crescendo when God acts sovereignly to protect both the child and his parents by opening the door for them to leave town for a season. In short, God's solution to the threat posed by Herod is to instruct them to flee to a safe harbor area of the Roman Empire. Matthew tells us what happened next in Matthew 2:13-15:

¹³After they had gone, an angel of the Lord appeared to Joseph in a dream. "Get up, take the child and his mother, and flee to Egypt," he said. "Stay there until I tell you, because Herod intends to search for the child and kill him." ¹⁴So Joseph got up, took the child and his mother, and left at night for Egypt. ¹⁵He stayed there until Herod's death in order to fulfill what was declared by the Lord through the prophet when he said, "Out of Egypt I called my Son."

The angel Gabriel appeared to Mary in a direct visitation. This wasn't the case with respect to Joseph. For one thing, the angel who communicated to Joseph isn't named precisely. A linguistic ambiguity in the Greek language of Matthew's Gospel narrative leaves room for the possibility that verse thirteen should be read as "…the angel of the Lord appeared to Joseph" in the dream that he had that night.

If this verse is rendered as "*the* angel of the Lord" rather than "an angel of the Lord," the reason why this being is not named would have been self-evident to any devout Jew who met him, whether in a dream, in a vision, or in a direct visitation: this would have been God himself, visiting Joseph as "the Angel who is the Lord." This rendering is the grammatical implication of the Hebrew *genitive of apposition*[3] that comprises the title for God in the Hebrew Scriptures when he visits human beings in order to communicate with them directly through visions, dreams, or visitations. In short, even while Jesus was incarnate in mortal human flesh, his omnipotent and omniscient deity could act with the same limitless capabilities that he displayed when he visited Abraham just before he judged Sodom and Gomorrah, when he warned a pagan king in a dream not to mess with Abraham's wife, or when he visited countless other individuals throughout biblical history.

6. Bethlehem's Pain Inflicted (Matthew 2:16-18)

In their obedience to God's clear directive to leave town, a number of innocent lives were lost due to Herod's malicious choice to act out his personal paranoia in order to protect his throne. Matthew 2:16-18 informs us:

> [16]*Herod flew into a rage when he learned that he had been tricked by the wise men, so he ordered the execution of all the male children in Bethlehem and all its neighboring regions, who were two years old and younger, according to the time that he had determined from the wise men.* [17]*Then what was declared by the prophet Jeremiah was fulfilled when he said,*
> [18]*"A voice was heard in Ramah:*
> *wailing and great mourning.*
> *Rachel was crying for her children.*
> *She refused to be comforted,*
> *because they no longer existed."*

---

3   A *genitive of apposition* is a grammatical device in which a noun is followed by another noun in the possessive case, by which the following noun is a rephrasing of the first noun. A modern example of this structure can be seen in the phrase *city of Chicago*. By this term, the person who uses it is referring to "the city that is also known as Chicago." So also with the term "the angel of the Lord": it means "the angel who is also known as the Lord."

The town referred to by Matthew's Gospel has been identified with the modern *Nevi Shmuel* (named after the prophet Samuel). This neighborhood lies about four or five miles to the northwest of modern Jerusalem. Its precise location remains unknown today, however.

If the Ramah referred to in Matthew 2:18 is the same village noted above, then it was the hometown of Samuel's father Elkanah (cf. 1 Samuel 2:11; 7:17) and is frequently referred to in the Old Testament's stories relating to that prophet and to narratives that mention King David (cf. 1 Samuel 15:34, 16:13, and 19:18-23). The prophet Samuel was buried in Ramah (cf. 1 Samuel 25:1). A school of New Testament thought dating from the twelfth century has suggested that Ramathaim Zofim also may be identified with Arimathea, the hometown of Joseph, who owned the tomb in which Jesus was laid to rest after his death by crucifixion.[4]

ON THE UNIQUE REFERENCES TO RAMAH IN THE NEW TESTAMENT

Some liberal higher critics of the New Testament text have suggested over the years that this horrific event (also referred to as the *Slaughter of the Innocents*) never actually occurred. These scholars have labeled Matthew's narrative an instance of creative hagiography,[5] by which they mean a fictional biography. But these higher critics ignore the following facts:

First, the reason why Matthew's Gospel is the only narrative regarding Jesus' life pertains to the perspective of Matthew's writing. As we noted in our observations concerning the Gospel of Matthew starting on page 14 of this book, Matthew wrote to the Jews, portraying Jesus as the rightful king of Israel. Mark, Luke, and John wrote with differing motivations and purposes. Their accounts do not *contradict* Matthew; they only *supplement* his work with differing (but not conflicting) perspectives. The genealogy of Jesus included at the beginning of the Gospel of Matthew was included

---

4   As claimed by Petrus Comestor (ca. 1100-1179) in his Historia Scholastica, Cap. CLXXX: De sepultura Domini. For further reading, see https://en.wikipedia.org/wiki/Ramathaim-Zophim.

5   See, for example, Geza Vermes, *The Nativity: History and Legend*, London, Penguin, 2006, page 22 and E. P. Sanders, *The Historical Figure of Jesus*, Penguin, 1993, page 85.

as part of Matthew's testimony concerning Jesus' right to rule over Judah. It is expected that his Gospel would include narratives such as the incident regarding Herod's paranoid response to the Messiah's rightful claim to the throne. Also, Matthew's account of the life of Jesus contains embedded within it an undeniable focus on *fulfilled prophecy*. Accordingly, it seems entirely appropriate that the incident would be recorded solely by Matthew.

Second, the actual number of innocent children put to death at the direct order of Herod was probably not very high—and it's almost certain that the total was not high enough to warrant a permanent story being circulated within the annals of Roman history. The respected historian Josephus does not mention the event in his classic work *Antiquities of the Jews*, which he probably composed ca. 94 AD. Given the history of Herod's various assassinations that he ordered, the story's absence may be attributable to it not rising to the level of the macabre that would warrant Josephus mentioning in his writings. Frankly, the story is *entirely consistent* with the known monstrous character of that despot Herod.

If Bethlehem at the time of Jesus' second year of life consisted of about 1,000 people, it is not unreasonable to suggest that the total number of infants killed was about two dozen or so.

Third, liberal higher critics who deny the historical accuracy of the event, or who deny that it ever occurred at all, are ignoring the plain evidence of history. For example, the late fourth century apparently pagan writer Macrobius Ambrosius Theodosius records in his work *Saturnalia*:

> *When he [Emperor Augustus] heard that among the boys in Syria under two years old whom Herod, king of the Jews, had ordered killed, his own son was also killed, he said: it is better to be Herod's pig, than his son.*

By the way, this quote from Macrobius contains an oft-repeated, wicked pun that reflects a Greek origin for the proverb. The Greek word for "pig" (*hous*) bears a close linguistic assonance with the Greek word for "son" (*houios*)—the two words are nearly identical in pronunciation, the two words rising almost (but not quite) to the level of being *homophones*. For a first century AD observer to remark that it was better to be Herod's pig than his son would have constituted an incident of wicked, cynical, gallows humor.

Fourth, there's a high likelihood that one of the motivations that drives liberal higher critical skepticism is an understandable, if dubious, response to ecclesiastical *exaggeration* that has taken place over the centuries regarding the Slaughter of the Innocents. Byzantine scholarship estimated that about 14,000 infants were slaughtered. The Syrian tradition suggests that the actual number was much higher, on the order of 64,000. And Coptic sources place the total at 144,000 (perhaps equating this number with the 144,000 *adult evangelists* from the twelve tribes described in the book of the Revelation to John). The view held by the Catholic Encyclopedia from the early 1900s is more realistic: it suggests that no more than twenty (and perhaps as few as about half a dozen) children were executed in Bethlehem itself, plus about a dozen more in the surrounding suburbs:

> *The Greek Liturgy asserts that Herod killed 14,000 boys* (ton hagion id chiliadon Nepion*), the Syrians speak of 64,000, many medieval authors of 144,000, according to Apocalypse 14:3. Writers who accept the historicity of the episode reduce the number considerably, since Bethlehem was a rather small town. Joseph Knabenbauer brings it down to fifteen or twenty* (Evang. S. Matt., I, 104*), August Bisping to ten or twelve* (Evang. S. Matt.*), Lorenz Kellner to about six* (Christus und seine Apostel, Freiburg, 1908*)* [6]

If the view of the Catholic Encyclopedia is accurate, the comparatively small number of children killed would account for it being ignored by the secular historians of subsequent centuries: frankly, the story would not have been newsworthy in their estimation when compared with Herod's other atrocities.

---

6   Cited from Catholic Encyclopedia; cf. *Anzeiger kath. Geistlichk. Deutschl.*, 15 February 1909, p. 32. For further reading, see http://ww.newadvent.org/cathen/07419a.htm. And see https://en.wikipedia.org/wiki/Massacre_of_the_Innocents.

Fifth, liberal higher critics of Matthew's narrative ignore the ancient historical account that refers to the incident in Bethlehem contained in the apocryphal work *Protoevangelium of James*, which has been dated to ca. 150 AD, about a century after Matthew would have recorded his Gospel. While the *Protoevangelium* does not include Matthew's record of the flight into Egypt, it does provide a fascinating insight into the story from the standpoint of John the Baptizer. At the time of the Bethlehem massacre, John the Baptizer would have been at an age that could have rendered him eligible to be included in Herod's execution order. The *Protoevangelium of James* records this incident, thus providing one explanation regarding how John the Baptizer escaped execution:

> *And when Herod knew that he had been mocked by the Magi, in a rage he sent murderers, saying to them: Slay the children from two years old and under. And Mary, having heard that the children were being killed, was afraid, and took the infant and swaddled Him, and put Him into an ox-stall. And Elizabeth, having heard that they were searching for John, took him and went up into the hill-country, and kept looking where to conceal him. And there was no place of concealment. And Elizabeth, groaning with a loud voice, says: O mountain of God, receive mother and child. And immediately the mountain was cleft, and received her. And a light shone about them, for an angel of the Lord was with them, watching over them.*[7]

7. JOSEPH'S DIRECTION CONFIRMED (MATTHEW 2:19-21)

Matthew's narrative regarding the visit of the Magi concludes by jumping forward a few years. Matthew writes in Matthew 2:19-21:

> *[19]But after Herod died, an angel of the Lord appeared in a dream to Joseph in Egypt. [20]"Get up," he said. "Take the child and his mother, and go to the land of Israel, because those who were trying to kill the child are dead."*
> *[21]So Joseph got up, took the child and his mother, and went into the land of Israel.*

---

[7] Cited from http://www.newadvent.org/fathers/0847.htm. See especially ¶22.

God sent Joseph, Mary, and Jesus back to Israel a number of years later. Exactly how long the family sojourned in Egypt isn't recorded, thus giving rise to secular myths about Jesus to the effect that during this time, Jesus learned all manner of Egyptian sorcery and shamanism from various teachers of the occult who wandered into his life under Mary and Joseph's apparent tutorage. But this "solution" to where Jesus obtained the miraculous powers that he never displayed until *after* he began his public ministry at about the age of thirty is not supported by any manuscript evidence, whether within or outside of the New Testament records.

8. GOD'S WORD FULFILLED (MATTHEW 2:22-23)

It would appear from our eighth observation that we can glean from the fourth spiritual test question that Mary was being tasked with facing when dealing with the challenges involved in surrendering her illusion of personal security to the God who had great plans for her and her son that God can use that old wise proverb "Like father, like son" to accomplish his sovereign will on earth. Notice what Matthew's record in Matthew 2:22-23 tells us about what came about a few years after Joseph, Mary, and Jesus had lived for a while in Egypt;

> *22But when he heard that Archelaus was ruling over Judea in place of his father Herod, he was afraid to go there, after having been warned in a dream. So he left for the region of Galilee 23and settled in a town called Nazareth in order to fulfill what was said by the prophets: "He will be called a Nazarene."*

No matter what else we might say about Mary's husband Joseph, we *cannot* say that he was one who had a tendency to ignore God whenever he spoke to him. While the record of the New Testament does not record a single instance in which the man has even *one word to say*, whether to God or to his fellow human beings, the bottom line is that he was sensitive to the directions that were to be given him by God.

Along the way, God used the man's natural reaction that anybody would have to receiving bad news via a direct premonition and warning from God himself: Joseph became afraid. That fear was the hinge point around which Joseph and his family was guided to move from Egypt, not to Bethlehem, where they had resided for a season before they had left as refugees to Egypt, but rather back to the comparative safety of Nazareth.

CONCLUDING THOUGHTS: ON AVERTED DISASTER: HOW TO RESPOND WHEN GOD SHOWS YOU THAT HE ISN'T THROUGH WITH YOU YET...

Mary passed her fourth spiritual challenge with flying colors. She trusted in God that his larger plan for her life (and for his plans for Jesus and for her husband Joseph's life) would reach its objective despite the dangers that would come into her life. She came within a few hours of seeing her son die by execution at the age of about two years, and God preserved Jesus' life until the time would come more than thirty years later when he would lay down his life as a ransom for many.

Let's conclude our study of Mary's fourth test question by repeating our first inquiry that we set forth as we began this chapter: Have you ever found yourself in a situation in which you might easily have died or have been critically injured, but you somehow survived? Maybe in your case you were involved in an automobile or other vehicle accident. Maybe you were the object of a vicious physical assault. Perhaps you were attacked by a vicious spouse, by another relative, or by an acquaintance. Maybe you contracted what could have been an otherwise critical or fatal illness, or maybe you gave into despair and attempted suicide.

No matter what you went through, one of the lessons you can take away from studying this fourth test question that Mary faced is that you have the assurance from this passage that when you've survived a close call with death, God isn't through with you and your life yet. He has more in store for you, and he invites you to interpret the trauma that affected you so deeply as his clear and present communication that he will surely finish in your life what he has begun.

105

TEST #5:
WILL YOU GIVE YOUR MOST IMPORTANT POSSESSIONS TO GOD?

YOUR CHILDREN DON'T BELONG TO YOU...

Let's be honest about our own children: all too often we think they belong to us for the pragmatically simple reason that we brought them into the world, but the truth is that we're only *stewards* of them for a season until they have come to an age at which they're capable of assuming the responsibilities of life in the human community as adult, productive residents of the world. This daunting fact is especially applicable to God's people, who are tasked with raising their children in the way that is appropriate for them.

For Jews living in the first century, Israel's community of faith had *for generations* required all young people to assume the responsibilities of adulthood upon the commencement of the thirteenth year following their birth. These responsibilities, as we noted earlier in our studies, could be entered into voluntarily at any time during the young person's twelfth year. In the case of Jesus, Mary and Joseph clearly considered Jesus to be mature enough to accept these responsibilities earlier in his life rather than later.

Frankly, one of the most important and strategically significant challenges we face in our life of faith is seen in how we respond to the fifth spiritual test question that Mary the mother of Jesus was tasked to answer right about the time it became incumbent upon the youthful incarnate son of God to assume his responsibilities as an adult in Israel's community of faith during the first century, AD. Mary was, in essence, asked the important question, "Will you give your most important treasure into the care and custody of God?" The story of Mary's fifth spiritual test is recorded for us in Luke 2:41-52. In looking at this short narrative, I've been able to divide the story into four component elements.

1. AN OUTWARDLY ORDINARY EVENT LEADS TO AN INWARDLY IMPORTANT TEST (LUKE 2:41-45)

Mary's fifth test question occurred in the midst of what would for most Israelis living in the first century AD appear to be merely routine and outwardly ordinary. Luke's Gospel describes what happened:

> *[41]Every year Jesus' parents would go to Jerusalem for the Passover Festival. [42]When Jesus was twelve years old, they went up to the festival as usual. [43]When the days of the festival were over, they left for home. The young man Jesus stayed behind in Jerusalem, but his parents did not know it. [44]They thought that he was in their group of travelers. After traveling for a day, they started looking for him among their relatives and friends. [45]When they did not find him, they returned to Jerusalem, searching desperately for him.*

As we noted earlier in this work, nobody knows with any certainty the time of year when Jesus was born in Bethlehem. The traditional date of 25 December is somewhat problematic. If we consider the possibility that the New Testament's statement that Mary visited Elizabeth during Elizabeth's sixth month of her pregnancy, and if we assume that Elizabeth conceived in January, as the linguistic ambiguity of the New Testament tantalizingly suggests, it would place the termination date for Mary's pregnancy somewhere around Passover of the following year, making Jesus' *possible* birthday falling near (if not directly on) Passover. If this thesis is correct, it means that Jesus was being brought to the Temple in the City of David in order to celebrate his *bar mitzvah* on or about his twelfth birthday.

But for Mary (and for Joseph, too), this happy celebration will briefly turn rather ominous. Traveling from Nazareth to Jerusalem for Passover would have entailed Mary, Joseph, and their family making their journey as part of a larger entourage that would visit Jerusalem as a group. Think of the ancient first century equivalent of a tour group going on a religious holiday and you won't be far off the mark.

In the confusion of the trip, Mary and Joseph immersed themselves in (and, apparently, became rather distracted by) all of the myriads of details that must have accompanied the responsibilities of Passover travel. By Jesus' twelfth year, no doubt some of the brothers and sisters of Jesus that are mentioned in the New Testament had come along, which would have entailed Mary and Joseph becoming preoccupied with the needs of their younger children. So it's not really surprising that Jesus got misplaced, so to speak, in the confusion.

HOW WOULD *YOU* REACT IF YOU MISPLACED THE SON OF GOD?

Looking back at the incident from the viewpoint of 2,000 years later and counting, we're tempted to chuckle briefly as we read what happened. Have you ever known someone who accidentally left their mother-in-law behind in the restroom of a gas station? I know a few people who accidentally lost one of their children in a museum in Washington, DC. (To tell the whole truth, it was my own parents who did the losing, and the son they misplaced was my younger brother when he was about eight years old.)

In the case of Mary and Joseph, they misplaced the son of God for about three days. Little did Mary and Joseph know it at the time, but the incident would turn out to be an excellent object lesson of faith that would be passed down from year to year for centuries as the only information about the childhood of Jesus that has survived the centuries in order for us to read it today. After this date, any mention of Jesus and his family disappear completely from the New Testament record until he turns about thirty years old.

2. AN OUTWARDLY INNOCENT OCCASION CONTAINS AN INWARDLY ESSENTIAL LESSON (LUKE 2:46-48)

Eventually, Mary and Joseph located their son, who apparently had stayed behind in the Temple complex in order to listen to the various rabbinic leaders as they taught their lessons to everyone who made an appearance. Do note, though, that this apparently innocent event contained within it an essential lesson for Jesus' parents; specifically, that Jesus was fully aware of what God's plan for his life would entail as he entered into Israel's first century community of faith. Luke writes:

> *46 Three days later, they found him in the Temple sitting among the teachers, listening to them, and posing questions to them. 47 All who heard him were amazed at his intelligence and his answers. 48 When Jesus' parents saw him, they were shocked. His mother asked him, "Son, why have you treated us like this? Your father and I have been worried sick looking for you!"*

3. A DIRECT RESPONSE FROM THE MESSIAH COMMUNICATES THE TEST'S MEANING (LUKE 2:49)

My colleague Dr. Chuck Missler at the Koinonia House base in Reporoa, New Zealand is fond of remarking that his favorite quotation from American author Mark Twain is that the two most important days of an individual's life are *first*, the day that person is born, and *second* the day on which that individual discovers *why* he or she was born. The incident that occurred in the life of Jesus during his twelfth year clearly communicates the priority that Mary is being asked to place on her stewardship over her supernaturally conceived son.

Notice, if you would please, how Jesus *completely ignores* Mary's accusing question, "Why have you treated us like this?" Now at this juncture, we should take a moment to point out that in the cultural milieu of first century Israel, this reply in the form of Jesus' question carries absolutely no disrespect or callous indifference to his parents' concerns. He merely asked them in reply to their question why they hadn't been faithful in regards to the information they already had about him as he grew up in their presence during the previous eleven years. Luke records Jesus' two sentence response, which consisted of two questions posed to Mary and her husband:

> [49]*He asked them, "Why were you looking for me? Didn't you know that I had to be in my Father's house?"*

I'm not inclined to suggest at this juncture that Jesus was rebuking them on any level at all. He was stimulating them to think through what was really behind their questions. In essence, I suspect that Jesus was interpreting the occasion to remind them that it had always been his spiritual priority to congregate in his Father's house, the Temple. He was reminding his own parents that they were stewards over Jesus for a short season of life only, and that their responsibility as parents was to facilitate Jesus becoming in his adulthood everything that had been predicted about him by the angel Gabriel, by the shepherds who visited him the night of his birth, by Simeon and Anna at the occasion of his dedication on the 40th day of his life, and by the visiting Magi toward the beginning of his second year.

4. OBEDIENCE OF FAITH EVEN IN THE MIDST OF SPIRITUAL AND MENTAL CONFUSION (LUKE 2:50-51)

It is to the credit of the young Jesus of Nazareth that even at the tender age of twelve years, he was willing to meet his parents within the limits of their faith and at the point and level of their own understanding. Notice, if you would, how Luke explains that Jesus' reply to Mary's anxious questioning, though misunderstood by his parents, resulted in Jesus remaining in complete submission to the authority of his parents. Luke writes:

> *[50] But they did not understand what he told them. [51] Then he went back with them, returning to Nazareth and remaining in submission to them. His mother continued to treasure all these things in her heart.*

We should also remember at this point that Mary herself wasn't much older than the age of 12 years when God caught Mary's attention by the angelic visitation of Gabriel himself. We're inclined to suggest that her remembrance of this occasion may have been reflected in her treasuring in her heart the response of Jesus to the questions that Mary and Joseph had asked Jesus. To sum up, Mary's inward pondering of Jesus' reply to Mary's question serves as our indicator that she did not consider Jesus's explanation (presented as it was in the form of the two questions that he asked) to be rebellious on any level. Quite the opposite, Luke 2:50-51 gives us a not-so-subtle hint that Mary had passed her fifth spiritual test by answering the question, "Are you willing to entrust your greatest treasure into the care and custody of God's plan?" with a resounding "Yes!"

CONCLUSION: GOD USES SUCCESSFUL TESTS TO ACCOMPLISH HIS WILL (LUKE 2:52)

Notice, if you would please, how as a follow-on to the story of how Mary has passed her fifth test with flying colors, Luke reminds us that:

⁵²Meanwhile, Jesus kept on growing wiser and more mature, and in favor with God and his fellow man.

We're inclined to suggest as we close our study of Mary's fifth test question that God wove into Jesus' personal preparation for his life's work her and Joseph's positive response to the fifth test question posed to them both. He continued to perfect his growing maturity and wisdom, all the while growing in grace and favor with his fellow believers and with his own family.

TEST #6:
HOW WILL YOU BEAR THE LOSS
OF YOUR SPOUSE?

DID MARY BECOME A SINGLE PARENT WIDOW?

We concede at the outset of our discussion of Mary's sixth spiritual challenge to her faith that our listing of the probable death of Mary's husband Joseph is a purely theoretical observation. That's because most Biblical scholars conclude that sometime after the Gospel narratives mention him at the time of his visit with Mary and Jesus to Jerusalem in order to celebrate Passover during Jesus' twelfth year, Joseph disappears almost completely from the New Testament narratives.

For example, the lack of reference to Joseph can be seen in Matthew 13:54-57 and Mark 6:1-3. Notice how the people who lived in Jesus' adopted hometown of Nazareth *omit* mentioning

Joseph's name when they confronted him about teaching in the main synagogue located in that city. Matthew writes in Matthew 13:54-57:

> *53 When Jesus had finished these parables, he left that place.*
> *54 He went to his hometown and began teaching the people in their synagogue in such a way that they were amazed and asked, "Where did this man get this wisdom and these miracles? 55 This is the builder's son, isn't it? His mother is named Mary, isn't she? His brothers are James, Joseph, Simon, and Judas, aren't they? 56 And his sisters are all with us, aren't they? So where did this man get all these things?" 57 And they were offended by him.*

They only refer to Jesus as "*the builder's son*," without mentioning Joseph's name. As native residents of Nazareth, surely they would have known Joseph's name. By leaving his name out of their criticism, some scholars suggest that they're ignoring the man's name out of polite respect for the dead. At any rate, Matthew's narrative has its parallel in Mark 6:1-3, where we read that the term "the builder" is not used to refer to Joseph, but rather *to Jesus himself*:

> *1 Jesus left that place and went back to his hometown, and his disciples followed him. 2 When the Sabbath came, he began to teach in the synagogue, and many who heard him were utterly amazed. "Where did this man get all these things?" they asked. "What is this wisdom that has been given to him? What great miracles are being done by his hands! 3 This is the builder, the son of Mary, and the brother of James, Joseph, Judas, and Simon, isn't it? His sisters are here with us, aren't they?" And they were offended by him.*

It has been suggested that the reason why Jesus is called "the builder" along with Joseph is because, consistent with the cultural traditions of his day, Jesus would most likely have been trained in a trade of some kind. The usual candidate for Jesus to have adopted as his own trade would have been the occupation engaged in by his step-father Joseph. (By the way, the Greek word that is usually translated as the term "carpenter" in the Gospel narratives more accurately should be translated as "builder." The Greek word τέκτων (*téktōn*) describes one who constructs buildings. Think of a modern construction contractor rather than a wood worker and you won't be far off the mark in picturing what Joseph and Jesus did for their employment.)

Joseph is not mentioned as being present during the crucifixion of Jesus. No Gospel narrative mentions him as being in attendance at the execution of his son. Catholic tradition suggests that Joseph was significantly older than Mary when he married her, and therefore Roman Catholic dogma teaches that Joseph died of old age or other natural causes sometime after Jesus attained his twelfth birthday. Catholics further suggest that the brothers and sisters mentioned in the narratives above refer to children that Joseph brought to his marriage with Mary from a previous marriage, but that his first wife had passed away. (The identity of this alleged first wife is not revealed in Catholic tradition.)

Strictly speaking, however, there is no textual support for this tradition that Joseph had been married before, that he brought previously sired children into his relationship with Mary, or that he was significantly older than Mary. All of these suggestions are *speculation*, and seem from the viewpoint of Protestants to have been crafted as a means to provide an explanation as to how the Catholic view that Mary never had any children with Joseph could sustain credibility. The official Catholic view of Mary is that she never had any other children other than Jesus himself, and that she remained a perpetual virgin for the remainder of her life after Jesus was born. There is no direct New Testament evidence for this view.

A CONTRARIAN THEORY: WAS JOSEPH STILL ALIVE AT THE BEGINNING OF JESUS' MINISTRY?

A contrarian view that denies Joseph's supposed early death is supported by a few references to him in the New Testament's Gospel narratives. For example, consider how Philip addresses Jesus in John 1:43-45 as the son of the apparently still living Joseph:

> *[43]...Jesus decided to go away to Galilee, where he found Philip and told him, "Follow me."[44]Now Philip was from Bethsaida, the hometown of Andrew and Peter.*
> *[45]Philip found Nathaniel and told him, "We have found the man about whom Moses in the Law and the Prophets wrote—Jesus, the son of Joseph, from Nazareth."*
> *[46]Nathaniel asked him, "From Nazareth? Can anything good come from there?"*

The implication of this referral to Joseph suggests that the man was still alive at the beginning of Jesus' call to discipleship of his first followers.

Philip's reference to Joseph isn't the only time people living in Israel during the time of Jesus ministry had no apparent knowledge that Joseph had died. See, for example, John 6:41-42; which mentions the people who lived in Capernaum. This passage from John's Gospel is clearly referring to Jesus as the son of an apparently still living Joseph:

> *[41]Then the Jewish leaders began grumbling about him because he said, "I am the bread that came down from heaven."*
> *[42]They kept saying, "This is Jesus, the son of Joseph, isn't it, whose father and mother we know? So how can he say, 'I have come down from heaven'?"*

Notice, if you would please, how both Jesus' father *and* mother are referred to as being known *in the present tense*. For those of our readers who are knowledgeable about Greek grammar, we invite you to notice the present tense form of the verb οἶδα (*oîda*) "to know" that is found in verse 42:

Οὐχ οὗτός ἐστιν Ἰησοῦς ὁ υἱὸς Ἰωσήφ, οὗ ἡμεῖς οἴδαμεν τὸν πατέρα καὶ τὴν μητέρα;

The verb form οἴδαμεν (*oídamen*) that appears in the grammatical structure of this sentence must be applied with *equal* weight and hermeneutical emphasis on both objects of the verb; that is, to both

Joseph *and* Mary equally. In simple terms, if they're saying "we know Mary," whom all scholars admit was still alive at the time the incident noted in John 6:42 occurred, then Joseph must have been still alive at the same time period.

In fairness to opposing views that suggest Joseph had already died by the time the event in John 6:41-42 occurred, it's possible that the verb οἴδαμεν (*oídamen*) is a reference to their present knowledge of Joseph's and Mary's *reputation in the community* rather than their actual *status as living individuals*. Enough ambiguity exists, both in the grammatical structure of the text and also in the cultural milieu of first century Israel to make a precise conclusion problematic.

Considered as a whole, though, the overall evidential picture seems to argue rather strongly that Joseph had passed away at some point in time during the early adulthood period of Jesus' life.

The Attitude of Jesus Regarding Widows

If for the sake of our study of the life of Mary we assume that she suffered the loss of her husband Joseph at some point in Jesus' early adulthood (that is, at some period *after* he attained his twelfth birthday), significant insights can be gained regarding the ministry of Jesus to widows and their children. That's because as a young man reaching full maturity within the context of being raised by a single parent widow, Jesus displayed considerable human empathy with regard to the challenges faced by Mary as she responded to God's sixth spiritual test question, "How will you bear the loss of your spouse?"

To put things rather succinctly, Jesus had a special place in his heart and ministry to widows and the fatherless. Could it be that part of this empathy stems from his mother becoming a widow unexpectedly, with the result that Jesus was an *orphan*, along with his brothers and sisters mentioned in the Gospels?

Despite the tendency of Jesus' brothers and sisters to disbelieve that he was the Messiah during the years of his mortality, nevertheless we can posit that even in his pre-public ministry years, a heart for widows and their children was evident to his family, as evidenced by a comment made in later years by Jesus' younger brother, who composed the letter of James that comprises one of the books of the New Testament. James 1:27 records one of the more practical summaries in the Bible regarding what constitutes true faith in God. He defined the Christian faith with these words:

> *[27]A religion that is pure and stainless according to God the Father is this: to take care of orphans and widows who are suffering, and to keep oneself unstained by the world.*

JESUS EMPATHIZED WITH SINGLE PARENTS

Consider, if you would please, the following examples from the Gospel narratives that illustrate the special empathy displayed by Jesus in his ministry focus on the needs of widows. For one thing, notice how Jesus displayed knowledge of what it means for a poverty-stricken widow to give generously out of her need to God and his work. Mark 12:41-44 tells us about what happened one day when Jesus was visiting the Temple:

> *[41]As Jesus sat facing the offering box, he watched how the crowd was dropping their money into it. Many rich people were dropping in large amounts. [42]Then a destitute widow came and dropped in two small copper coins, worth about a cent. [43]He called his disciples and told them, "I tell all of you with certainty, this destitute widow has dropped in more than everyone who is contributing to the offering box, [44]because all of them contributed out of their surplus, but out of her poverty she has given everything she had to live on."*

The incident is also referred to in Luke's narrative of the Gospels. Luke 21:1-4 tells us:

> *[1]Now Jesus looked up and saw rich people dropping their gifts into the offering box. [2]Then he saw a destitute widow drop in two small copper coins. [3]He said, "I tell you with certainty, this destitute widow has dropped in more than all of them, [4]because all the others contributed to the offering out of their surplus, but she, in her poverty, dropped in everything she had to live on."*

We'll have more to say about the example of a widow giving to God everything she had to live on when we look at the single parent of Zarephath, below.

JESUS' EMPATHY WITH THE WIDOW OF NAIN

We suspect that one of the reasons the New Testament records so many instances of Jesus' intervention on behalf of widows is founded in his empathy with his own mother's experiences raising him and his siblings without the benefits of having Joseph present in her life. Consider, for example, the story recorded in Luke's Gospel. Luke 7:11-17 presents the story:

> *[11] …Jesus went to a city called Nain. His disciples and a large crowd were going along with him. [12]As he approached the entrance to the city, a man who had died was being carried out. He was his mother's only living son, and she was a widow. A large crowd from the city was with her. [13]When the Lord saw her, he felt compassion for her.*

In examining this passage, we invite you to observe how Luke, who was trained as a physician in the finest medical traditions of his day, paid special attention to *the compassion of Jesus* to this widow in relation to her only living son. Luke informs us that "When the Lord saw her, he felt compassion for her." That he acted out of that compassion is self-evident from the resulting decision on his part to raise the woman's son from the dead. Luke 7:13b-17 sets forth the rest of the story:

> *He told her, "You can stop crying." [14]Then he went up and touched the bier, and the men who were carrying it stopped. He said, "Young man, I say to you, get up!" [15]The man who had been dead sat up and began to speak, and Jesus gave him back to his mother.*
> *[16]Fear gripped everyone, and they began to praise God. "A great prophet has appeared among us," they said, and "God has helped his people." [17]This news about Jesus spread throughout Judea and all the surrounding countryside.*

JESUS HATED ABUSIVE PRACTICES TOWARD WIDOWS

The clear message presented in the New Testament regarding Jesus' attitude toward the treatment of widows is that he had a very, very short temper when it came to this subject. Consider, for example, what Jesus had to say to the Pharisees in Matthew 23:14:

> *[14] "How terrible it will be for you, scribes and Pharisees, you hypocrites! You devour widows' houses and say long prayers to cover it up. Therefore, you will receive greater condemnation!*

This rebuke is reiterated by John Mark in Mark 12:38-40, where Jesus repeats the same thing, but this time he directs his remarks to the general populace who were following him:

> *[38] As he taught, he said, "Beware of the scribes! They like to walk around in long robes, to be greeted in the marketplaces, [39] and to have the best seats in the synagogues and the places of honor at banquets. [40] They devour widows' houses and say long prayers to cover it up. They will receive greater condemnation!"*

Luke repeats the rebuke in Luke 20:45-47:

> *[45] While all the people were listening, he told his disciples, [46] "Beware of the scribes! They like to walk around in long robes and love to be greeted in the marketplaces and to have the best seats in the synagogues and the places of honor at banquets. [47] They devour widows' houses and say long prayers to cover it up. They will receive greater condemnation!"*

The incident was considered significant enough by the New Testament compilers of the Gospel record of Jesus that all three synoptic writers included the story.

JESUS' ATTITUDE TOWARD JUSTICE FOR WIDOWS

Jesus knew what it must have felt like to be a widow who was the victim of abuse in the courts. Consider how one of his most significant teachings regarding the impartial justice of God is contrasted using a parable crafted from the corrupt judicial practices that were rampant in the courts of Jesus day. Luke 18:1-8 records the story:

> *¹Jesus told his disciples a parable about their need to pray all the time and never give up. ²He said, "In a city there was a judge who didn't fear God or respect people. ³In that city there was also a widow who kept coming to him and saying, 'Grant me justice against my adversary.' ⁴For a while the judge refused. But later, he told himself, 'I don't fear God or respect people, ⁵yet because this widow keeps bothering me, I will grant her justice. Otherwise, she will keep coming and wear me out.'"*
> *⁶Then the Lord added, "Listen to what the unrighteous judge says. ⁷Won't God grant his chosen people justice when they cry out to him day and night? Is he slow to help them? ⁸I tell you, he will give them justice quickly..."*

JESUS REMEMBERED HIS CARE FOR THE SINGLE PARENT OF ZAREPHATH

Jesus of Nazareth once displayed a special remembrance that harkened back to the time before his incarnation. In Luke 4:4-26, he mentions an historical event that happened during the ministry of Elijah the prophet, who served God during the regime of King Ahab. The occasion of the display was a rebuke Jesus gave to the residents of Nazareth, which he visited one day to address the local synagogue. Luke writes:

> *²⁴He added, "I tell all of you with certainty, a prophet is not accepted in his hometown. ²⁵I'm telling you the truth—there were many widows in Israel in Elijah's time, when it didn't rain for three years and six months and there was a severe famine everywhere in the land. ²⁶Yet Elijah wasn't sent to a single one of those widows except to one at Zarephath in Sidon.*

Now let's pause for a moment and think about this incident. Consider, if you would please, how Jesus refers to Elijah as a prophet who "wasn't sent to a single one" of the widows living during the lifetime of Elijah, which many Biblical scholars date to the ninth century BC. We would do well to pay special attention to the special and deliberate use by Jesus of *the passive voice* to describe the sending of Elijah to visit the single parent of Zarephath and how Elijah did not visit Jewish single parents during the famine.

WHY JESUS RARELY REFERRED TO HIMSELF USING THE FIRST PERSON PRONOUN

As we pointed out in our previous work, *I Jesus: an Autobiography*, in which we presented Jesus as he described himself, his purpose, his nature, and his mission:

Jesus was extraordinarily reluctant to refer to himself with first person pronouns when talking about his claimed divine attributes. He also rarely utilized active verbs when talking about his claims to be able to exercise divine authority. For example, notice Jesus' comments about himself in Mark 2:10:

"I want you to know that the Son of Man has authority on earth to forgive sins…"

Jesus does not say, "I want you to know that I have authority on earth to forgive sins…" To do so would create the appearance of arrogance. So he avoids creating an impression of presumption by referring to himself in the third person singular. In other places in the New Testament, the reader also will observe that when referring to his actions as God, Jesus will utilize passive verbs instead of employing the active voice. For example, consider this statement made by Jesus in Matthew 10:26-28 during an address he made to his followers about why it's important never to be afraid of those who persecute them:

[26] "So never be afraid of them, because there is nothing hidden that will not be revealed, and nothing secret that will not be made known. [27] What I tell you in darkness you must speak

in the daylight, and what is whispered in your ear you must shout from the housetops. [28] Stop being afraid of those who kill the body but can't kill the soul. Instead, be afraid of the one who can destroy both body and soul in hell."

In these four short sentences, Jesus is telling his followers that:

- *First*, nothing can be hidden forever, because he will uncover all things hidden, a power that only God possesses.
- *Second*, nobody can keep secrets from him, because he will reveal them, a power of omniscience that can be wielded only by God.
- *Third*, instead of fearing other people, the followers of Jesus should fear him, because he can destroy human beings in hell, a prerogative that only God possesses.

An observant reader of the New Testament Gospels will also note that in the records of his public dialogs, Jesus refers to his possession of divine attributes in an almost casual, off-handed way, displaying a matter-of-factness that, frankly speaking, is incongruous with respect to the man's obvious humility, his heart as a servant of humanity, and with respect to the astounding claims that are being made by these verbs in the passive voice, third person singular.

Jesus is saying: "I can destroy the ungodly in hell," and, "I will reveal all hidden and secret evil activities undertaken by the ungodly." And he makes these statements obliquely, with *humility*, almost as if he's sharing a secret that only a select few people are privileged to hear. We do not wish to appear indelicate here, but nowadays people who speak that way about themselves have a tendency to be placed in rubber rooms by court-ordered psychologists on the grounds of mental instability.

In a separate incident that is theologically related to the case of Jesus' claim to have authority to forgive sins discussed in Mark 2, an incident recorded in Luke 7:48-50 provides a significant insight concerning the dynamics that were at work in Jesus' comments about his authority to forgive. The context of the incident recorded by Luke concerns a conversation Jesus had with a woman during an evening meal:

[48] Then Jesus told her, "Your sins are forgiven!"
[49] Those who were at the table with them began to say among themselves, "Who is this man who even forgives sins?"
[50] But Jesus told the woman, "Your faith has saved you. Go in peace."

Those sitting at the table watching the interaction between Jesus and the woman whose actions had drawn their attention during the dinner concluded that there was something unusual about the person of Jesus himself.

In simple terms, what Jesus said to the woman would, in other circumstances, be considered the highest arrogance at least, and downright blasphemous at worse. His comments were out of school, out of place, and far out of the protocol of a dinner discussion. And yet there is a casualness, a presuppositional set of assumptions that pervades the character of Jesus as he talks casually to the woman. That casualness is the self-confidence displayed as he tells the woman, "Go in peace." He tells her something that only God can truly know (that her sins had been forgiven), even though the extension of forgiveness is something that only God can accomplish.

And therein lies the consternation expressed by the dinner guests. They knew that one of only three possible conclusions could be drawn from what Jesus was saying to the woman: either Jesus was committing blasphemy, or he was claiming to know a fact that only God could know, or that he was claiming to be God himself.

In light of the above, we suggest that Jesus is using oblique language to inform his listeners that it was Jesus himself, in his eternal pre-incarnate existence as the Angel of the LORD in his dealings with mankind, who did the sending of Elijah to visit the woman in Zarephath. More than eight *hundred years* later, subsequent to the events described in 1 Kings 17, this unnamed *Philistine widow* remains on the mind of God incarnate. Bluntly put, he is *still* thinking about her *centuries* after the events occurred that are recorded in the Hebrew Scriptures!

She must have had phenomenal character to have attracted such attention and to serve as an example of rebuke to Israel for their unbelief. Accordingly, the lessons we can learn from her are significant enough that the incident of the single parent of Zarephath warrants further study in our examination of Mary, the mother of Jesus.

LESSONS FOR LIFE FROM THE SINGLE PARENT OF ZAREPHATH

Some wag once defined "life" as what happens to you while you're making other plans. Just as when Elijah accepted the ministry of the prophetic during the reign of that apostate King Ahab, so also was the situation with Mary as she entered into her role in the culmination of God's work in preparing for the incarnation of his own son: neither one of them were given a guarantee that everything would go the way they expected things to go. All they were really promised is that God will work everything out to his glory and to our greater good at our latter end. As a practical illustration of this principle, let's take a close look at what happened one day in a little Gentile town called Zarephath when God worked out a very, very special prophecy just for the benefit of a young single parent and her little boy. Then we'll conclude this sixth test question that Mary was called upon to answer by considering some final thoughts…

LESSONS FOR LIFE FROM THE HISTORICAL SETTING (1 KINGS 17:1-6)

1. THE TIME WAS DIVINELY ORDERED (1 KINGS 17:1)

Through the prophetic ministry of Elijah (the meaning of whose name implies linguistically that he was a gentile convert to Judaism), God ordained the timing of the discipline that would come to Israel during the reign of Ahab. Notice how the writer of 1 Kings describes the occasion as being divinely ordered with respect to timing in 1 Kings 17:1:

> *¹Elijah the foreigner, who was an alien resident from Gilead, told Ahab, "As the Lord GOD of Israel lives, in whose presence I'm standing, there will be neither dew nor rain these next several years, except when I say so."*

2. THE PROVISION WAS DIVINELY ORDERED (1 KINGS 17:2-6)

We invite the reader to notice, also, how God has ordained the circumstances that those who depend on him will be provided for, even if God is involved in disciplining other disobedient believers. The writer of 1 Kings describes the occasion as being divinely ordered with respect to God's provision for Elijah in 1 Kings 17:2-6:

> *²Later, this message came to him from the LORD: ³"Leave here and go into hiding at the Wadi Cherith, where it enters the Jordan River. ⁴You will be able to drink from that brook, and I've commanded some crows to sustain you there." ⁵So Elijah left and did exactly what the LORD had told him to do—he went to live near the Wadi Cherith, where it enters the Jordan River. ⁶Crows would bring him bread and meat both in the morning and in the evening, and he would drink from the brook.*

Figure 23: Elijah in the Wilderness. Image source: http://laymanswatch.com/ images/elijah.jpg

There's nothing in this text to suggest that Elijah's supply of food by the ravens was anything more than crude survival rations.

Ravens are scavengers, and would have provided the equivalent to Elijah of what today we might call road kill. The brook was a seasonal river. Its water supply may well have been partially stagnant. Accordingly, it's reasonable to suppose that what Elijah had to eat and drink wasn't particularly of a gourmet variety. But it kept him alive for the first part of the time of scarcity that had been decreed for the land.

3. THE SCARCITY WAS DIVINELY ORDERED (1 KINGS 17:7)

Notice also how God has ordained the scarcity that came about as a direct consequence of the time of discipline being worked by God in urging other disobedient believers to return to him. The writer of 1 Kings describes the scarcity that came about as having been divinely ordered, along with the timing and the scarcity. 1 Kings 17:7 succinctly informs us:

⁷But after a while, the brook dried up because there had been no rain in the land.

Observe, if you would please, how Elijah's new troubles came about as a direct result of his participation with God in the prophetic ministry. Faithful though he was in doing what he had been commissioned to do, nevertheless the man was subject to the consequences of his prophetic ministry.

I suspect Mary's situation was like that. In our previous studies, we observed that after Mary demonstrated her willingness to surrender her life to God's purpose, and after she had proved willing to give God her expectations about how life would turn out for her, she faced multiple challenges and dangers that would pierce her soul with sorrow. Facing the death of her spouse would be one of these sorrows, and the death of her son Jesus was still in the future when the loss of Joseph came about in her life. The bottom line lesson here that we glean from the examples of Elijah and Mary is that sometimes when you do the right thing, you'll suffer temporary loss as a result.

Turning Tragedy to Triumph: Lessons for Life from the Cruse of Oil Incident (1 Kings 17:8-16)

1. God's Call to Service Often Comes in the Midst of our Deepest Poverty (1 Kings 17:8-9)

Please note how God employs the *past tense* as he describes to Elijah how he is going to work to provide for Elijah during the famine. He tells Elijah that he "has commanded" a widow to sustain him. 1 Kings 17:8-9 set the stage for us:

> *[8] Then this message came to him from the LORD: [9] "Get up, move to Zarephath in Sidon, and stay there. Look! I've commanded a widow to sustain you there."*

But from the standpoint of this unnamed widow, this sustenance has not yet occurred: it's still a non-existent future event about which she is, for the moment, completely ignorant. Nevertheless, in God's economy, his plans to provide for her future are described as if they've already occurred.

2. God's Provision Comes as We are Faithful to Give up the Certain for the Uncertain (1 Kings 17:10-11)

God has plans for Elijah and this Philistine unbeliever. By the time the complete story has unfolded, the single parent of Zarephath will be a believer by personal experience in the power of God to do the impossible. As the story begins, she appears to be just another unbelieving Philistine gentile. Notice how she is invited by Elijah to give up her certain future of despair for the comparatively uncertain future of trust in God. 1 Kings 17:10-11 explains how this worked out:

> *[10] So he got up and went to Zarephath. As he arrived at the entrance to the city, a widow was there gathering sticks. So he asked her, "Please, may I have some water in a cup so I can have a drink." [11] While she was on her way to get the water, he called out to her, "Would you please also bring me a piece of bread while you're at it?"*

At first glance, when we read this paragraph we might be tempted to accuse Elijah of presumption and insensitivity. Keep in mind, though, that Elijah had been informed by God himself that his support during the famine would from that day on be provided through a single parent woman who would be sent into his life. It's clear from these two verses that he had met the person whom God intended to use to supply the needs of them both. But the woman didn't know that, as yet.

3. SOONER OR LATER, THE TESTING OF FAITH WILL REVEAL OUR BITTER HEART AND OUR LACK OF LOVE FOR HIM (1 KINGS 17:12)

Sometimes, when God asks us to do what we know to be impossible, he is doing that so that as we recognize our own impoverishment, we can meet him at the point of his omnipotent supply. But this unnamed single parent doesn't see her situation that way. All she knows is that the circumstances of her life are so desperate that she wants to die. Notice how the woman's response to Elijah demonstrates the degree of her despair. 1 Kings 17:12 tells us:

> *12 "As the LORD your God lives," she replied, "I don't have so much as a muffin, just a handful of flour in a bowl and some oil left in a bottle. Now I'm going to find some sticks so I can cook a last meal for my son and for me. Then we're going to eat it and die."*

To put things succinctly, this woman is suicidal. A handful of flour and some oil left in a small bottle would constitute ingredients sufficient to make what in our economy today would be a few small crackers, and nothing more. There certainly weren't enough supplies to feed two adults and a small child for even a single meal.

Let us not underestimate the grievousness of her life situation. Nobody dies from eating a few crackers for dinner. They don't, that is, unless the cook has poisoned the crackers somehow. Given that this single parent woman plans to have her and her son die right after dinner that day, it's not a stretch of the imagination to conclude that she had planned what today would have been called the murder-suicide of herself and her young child. But God had other plans as he watched this woman suffer within the context of a life situation that has come about because God was disciplining the nation of Israel, a country toward which she had no allegiance.

Notice also how she refers to God as "the LORD your God" as she addresses Elijah. At this point, she has not yet received a personal calling from him to believe and follow God. But, as we shall see below, that day is on the horizon. The circumstances that will unfold over the next many months remaining in the three and a half years of famine will result in her coming into a personal faith and trust in the God of Elijah. At the end of the story, she will no longer refer to God as "the LORD your God," but rather as "the LORD".

4. GOD'S SUPPLY FOR US WILL MANIFEST AS WE MAKE HIS INTERESTS OUR FIRST PRIORITY (1 KINGS 17:13-15)

> ¹³But Elijah told her, "You can stop being afraid. Go and do
> what you said, but first make me a muffin and bring it
> to me. Then make a meal for yourself and for your son,
> ¹⁴because this is what the Lord GOD of Israel says: 'That jar
> of flour will not run out, nor will that bottle of oil become
> empty until the very day that the LORD sends rain on the
> surface of the ground.'"
> ¹⁵So she went out and did precisely what Elijah told her to do.
> As a result, Elijah, the widow, and her son were fed for days.

This woman did in desperation what several centuries later Mary, the mother of Jesus of Nazareth did: she cooperated with the will of God and did as she was directed.

5. THE FAITHFULNESS OF GOD IN KEEPING HIS WORD IS DEMONSTRATED TOWARD HIS PEOPLE AS WE, HIS PEOPLE, DO WHAT HE REQUIRES (1 KINGS 17:16)

The result was that she, her son, and Elijah the prophet were supplied with nourishment throughout the duration of the famine, as we read in 1 Kings 17:16:

16 The jar of flour never ran out and the bottle of oil never became empty, just as the LORD had promised through Elijah.

As I read through this first incident in the life of the single parent of Zarephath, I noticed the astonishing parallels between what happened to her and what Mary went through. Both women were challenged to participate in God's specific plan for their lives while God was working out his larger plans for his people. In the widow's case, her life situation was being *set up as a testimony* against unbelieving and disobedient people living in both Elijah's day and, centuries later, in Jesus' day. In Mary's day, God was preparing her generation for the birth and public ministry of the Messiah. And with respect to both women, their appropriate response to what God was asking them to do resulted in life turning in directions they never otherwise could have imagined or experienced.

TURNING UNEXPECTED LOSS INTO A LESSON FOR LIFE (1 KINGS 17:17-23)

Earlier in this work, we noted that life isn't linear. Its direction can change in a moment so that in mid-morning we head somewhere we never imagined and end the day in a situation we never could have imagined. In the case of Mary and the single parent of Zarephath, their days began like any other, but then they both suffered unexpected and paralyzing loss. The widow lost her only son, and Mary lost her husband to whom she looked for her support and nurture. Irrespective of any temporary setbacks to their faith that they may have endured, however, ultimately both Mary and the single parent of Zarephath passed their respective spiritual tests that had been appointed for them.

1. GOD OFTEN PROVIDES SUPERNATURALLY SO THAT HE CAN RECEIVE GLORY FROM WHAT TO US APPEARS TO BE UNEXPECTED TRAGEDY (1 KINGS 17:17)

17 Sometime later, the son of the woman who owned the house became ill. In fact, his illness became so severe that he died.

If you were that single parent widow tasked with raising that little boy who died, wouldn't you be angry at God? Maybe you'd be inclined to deny that he exists, or that if he did, you'd be inclined to think he had no care or involvement in your life. In the admittedly unusual case of this woman from Zarephath, however, she couldn't deny the obvious *continual supply* of her own daily needs by the supernatural had provision of God himself in accordance with the word of Elijah. After all, her little boy's last meal was supplied supernaturally by God's continuous, daily, and miraculous provision. I think that one of the questions—or maybe the question would have been framed as an *accusation*—would have been for her to ask this: "Why, God, would you bother to provide food for my family if you were going to cause my little one to die a few hours after he enjoyed a meal that came supernaturally from your hand?"

Discerning *Reason* vs. *Purpose*

When tragedy strikes, it's part of our nature to challenge God by shouting out "Why?" rather than to invite God to show you what his overriding purpose is for the trouble. Contrasting the responses to tragedy shown by the single parent widow of Zarephath with the response shown by Mary, the mother of Jesus, I'd like to suggest that whereas this gentile widow demanded to know from God the *reason why* she lost her son, Mary waited on God to demonstrate the *purpose* that he had in mind as she walked through the loss of her husband.

In studying the two different responses by these women, I'm reminded of a question asked one day by the disciples of Jesus as they quizzed him about why a specific man whom Jesus met one day had been born blind. The story is set forth for our reading in John 9:1-5:

> *¹As he was walking along, he observed a man who had been blind from birth. ²His disciples asked him, "Rabbi, who sinned, this man or his parents, that caused him to be born blind?"*

At this point, Jesus takes a moment before responding to their question in order to provide a correction to their abysmally bad theology. The presupposition of their question was false. They assumed that the man's blindness had come about as a result of divine discipline administered by God. In their spiritually limited and downright *superstitious* view of life, either the man's parents had sinned at some time in the past, with the result that God had punished their child for their sins, or the child had been born blind because he himself had sinned before birth.

Now as to this latter situation, I see the response of the disciples as springing from one of the following rationalizations: *first*, they believed that the man had sinned in the womb of his mother sometime after conception and before coming into the world; or, *second*, the disciples believed in reincarnation and that he had committed some evil action or actions in a previous life. Either way, the disciples *assumed* that the man's blindness was a result of punished sin.

With respect to the latter possibility that reincarnation explained the phenomenon, nothing in rabbinic theology of the first century manifests such a view. It was foreign to their theology. Accordingly, I doubt that this latter explanation is a credible one. But the question of whether a person could sin in the womb happened to be a hot theological topic of debate at the time. Notice how Jesus responds to the disciples' question:

> [3]*Jesus answered, "Neither this man nor his parents sinned."*

But after Jesus corrects their abysmally bad theology by rejecting their sophomoric presumptions, he instructs them that they should be asking God to show the *purpose* for the troubles of life. He responds:

> *"This happened so that God's work might be revealed in him.*
> [4]*I must do the work of the one who sent me while it is day.*
> *Night is approaching, when no one can work.* [5]*As long as I'm in the world, I'm the light of the world."*

INTERPRETING THE FUTURE IN LIGHT OF THE PAST

There are two aspects of our past that we do not control: *first*, we have no control over our genetics, and *second*, we do not have control over our past environment. As to genetics, we don't have a choice as to our gender, our racial makeup, and our innate intelligence. Furthermore, we have limited control over our temperament. Now as to our environment, we don't control the country and heritage of our birth, the time of our birth, our birth order, or of the basic circumstances in which we grew from childhood into adult responsibility.

In contrast to our past, which is complete and cannot be altered, there are two basic aspects of our present and future that we *can control*: we have complete control over *our interpretations* regarding what has happened to us, and *second*, we have complete control over *the choices we make* in light of those interpretations. The example set by the patriarch Joseph comes to mind as an illustration of these principles. He was not under control of his birth order as one of Jacob's younger children. He didn't control the choices of his jealous brothers. He didn't control his having been handed over to slavery, and from slavery into Pharaoh's dungeon. But he did control his interpretation and choices that sprang from what happened to him: he interpreted everything to be part of God's overruling plan to preserve life and he chose to forgive his brothers for their evil behavior toward him.

In the case of the single parent of Zarephath and of Mary, the mother of Jesus, both of these women were faced with the necessity of coming to grips with interpreting their deep emotional loss in light of God's purposes, and they were tasked with the obligation to make specific choices in light of that interpretation. To the credit of Mary, there's no evidence or record of her responding to the apparent loss of her husband Joseph in any negative way at all. But this cannot be said—at first—with respect to the single parent widow of Zarephath.

2. THE DISASTERS OF LIFE REVEAL THE FOUNDATIONS OF OUR MOTIVES IN LIFE (1 KINGS 17:18)

¹⁸ "What do we have in common, you man of God?" she accused Elijah. "You came to me so you could uncover my guilt! And you're responsible for the death of my son!"

Harboring a false sense of guilt eventually will breed a false sense of personal responsibility for tragedies that invade our lives. This is what happened to the single parent of Zarephath. There's no evidence in the text recorded by the ancient author of 1 Kings 17 that she had done anything wrong to attract the disciplinary judgment of God. In fact, there's plenty of evidence that she was beginning to trust in God to provide for her on a day-to-day basis.

And then all of a sudden—wham! Right out of the blue comes the lightning strike of unexpected tragedy. As a result, she makes not one, but *two* mistakes:

- *First*, she blames her son's death on her own misbehavior; and

- *Second*, she blames God (by blaming God's agent the prophet Elijah) as the ultimately responsible party.

Do note, if you would please, how it *never occurred to her* that she can't logically entertain both possibilities as rational explanations in her mind. The two possibilities are mutually contradictory.

3. GOD'S DELIVERANCE FROM DIFFICULTIES MANIFESTS AS WE GIVE HIM OUR FALLEN HOPES AND COMFORTS (1 KINGS 17:19)

The tragedy that befell the single parent of Zarephath came about while Elijah is living at the woman's house as her guest. Notice the gracious attitude displayed by Elijah in his response to the woman's anguish. He invites her to give her child to him, as God's agent. 1 Kings 17:19 relates what happened:

¹⁹ "Give me your son," he replied. Then he took him from her lap, carried him upstairs to the room where he lived, and laid him on his bed.

Now let's pause for a moment in our examination of the story to note that at this point in the story, neither Elijah nor the widow knew what would happen next. Nobody had ever come back from the dead before this unnamed gentile little boy was restored to his mother. That the child would be resuscitated from the dead had not yet occurred to Elijah, and it's obvious that the woman wasn't thinking about that possibility. And yet certainly the thought was in the back of both of their minds. Otherwise, I can see no reason why Elijah would take the little boy's body upstairs, unless somewhere in his thoughts was the perception that something supernatural was in the works. And I'm not persuaded that the single parent of Zarephath was ignorant of this possibility, too. Otherwise, it's difficult to understand why she would have allowed Elijah to do anything except act as part of a burial detail for her son.

4. Even the Most Spiritually Mature and Useful Need to Learn that God Loves to Write the Last Chapters of Life's Tribulations (1 Kings 17:20-23)

One of the final lessons that comes out of the incident is that even God's special prophet had to learn that our omnipotent God loves to bring a finish to life's tragedies with a surprise ending that honors his eternal character. 1 Kings 17:20-23 tells us:

> [20] *Then he called out to the Lord and asked him, "Lord my God, have you also brought evil to this dear widow with whom I am living as her guest? Have you caused the death of her son?"* [21] *Then he stretched himself three times and cried out to the Lord, "Lord my God, please cause the soul of this little boy to return to him."*
> [22] *The Lord listened to Elijah, and the soul of the little boy returned to him, and he revived.* [23] *Then Elijah took the little boy downstairs from the upper chamber back into the main house and delivered him to his mother. "Look," Elijah told her, "your son is alive."*

LESSONS FOR LIFE FROM MARY THE SINGLE PARENT

The sum and substance of Mary's sixth spiritual challenge was not whether or not she would bear the loss of her spouse. Everyone who is married is going to lose their spouse sooner or later through death. For Mary, as it was for the single parent widow who lived in Zarephath, the real issue that would manifest is that in times of trouble, God loves to do more than we could ever ask or think. 1 Kings 17:24 tells us:

> *[24] The woman responded to Elijah, "Now at last I've really learned that you are a man of God and that what you have to say about the LORD is the truth."*

The single parent of Zarephath emerges from the trial of her faith, of her hopes, and of her dreams for the future with the personal understanding and knowledge of God and his ways that is the entire point of the passage. Her testimony that "What you have to say about the LORD is the truth" becomes the central lesson for us regarding what happened.

In light of this lesson, is it any wonder that eight hundred years *after* these events, the God who sent Elijah to visit her *still has her on his mind* as he compares the gentile woman's faith to the unbelief rampant in Israel during his lifetime?

Test #7:
Will You Remember
Who Jesus Really Is?

When God Rescues from Life's Mundane Problems...

The seventh spiritual test question with which Mary was presented challenges us with the Apostle John's story about a wedding in the village of Cana that Jesus attended one day, along with his disciples. The event recorded by John reminds us that it's important not to think of Jesus as less than he is. Let's see why this is true as we continue our study of the spiritual tests that Mary endured as she lived life as the mother of the Messiah. You'll find the story recorded in the Gospel of John. It took place on the third day of the first week in which he began his public ministry.

INTRODUCTORY THOUGHTS ON THE NATURE OF MIRACLES

God does miracles every second of every minute, every minute of every hour, and every hour of every day, if you define a miracle as the activity of God to interfere with the natural course of the universe that he created. The Jewish rabbis have understood this basic principle for centuries, and have passed this knowledge down through the ages, encapsulating this truth in the words that are spoken in prayer before meals. Take for example, the rabbinic blessing that is traditionally recited before one partakes of wine:

בָּרוּךְ אַתָּה ה' אֱלֹקֵינוּ מֶלֶךְ הָעוֹלָם
בּוֹרֵא פְּרִי הַגָּפֶן

Baruch atah A-donay, Elo-heinu Melech Ha'Olam borei pri hagafen.
Blessed are You, L-rd our G-d, King of the universe, Who creates the fruit of the vine.[1]

The Jewish community of faith considered all of God's work in bringing forth the fruit of the wine to be a creative act. The same root verb used in Genesis 1:1 by Moses to describe the creation of the universe *out of nothing* בָּרָא (bara) is employed in the traditional prayer over wine that is spoken to God before consuming it. As a footnote to our discussion of this point, the Jews considered this prayer to be mandatory for recital before consuming all forms of grape juice, whether fermented or not. Accordingly, regardless of which view you hold concerning the turning of water into wine by Jesus (whether you claim he made non-alcoholic juice or fermented wine), the creation of this product was made by a divine act initiated by Jesus.

To sum up, the New Testament record of the first miracle performed by Jesus the Messiah occurred when he utilized his power and ability as God incarnate to change the fundamental nature of the water into the fruit of the vine. Now speaking of his ability to do this in his capacity as God incarnate in a human being, all Christians

---

1 Cited from http://www.chabad.org/library/article_cdo/aid/278538/jewish/Basic-Blessings-on-Food-Guide.htm.

teach that God changes water into wine every day. It's just that he uses grapevines, sunshine, nutrients in the soil where the grapevine has been planted, water, and the annual growing season where the vineyard is located to do this.

But for one time in the history of his dealings with planet earth, God circumvents the process. He eliminates the need for grapes, sunshine, soil, and time. He converts existing water that has been placed by the servants in the containers directly into wine, bypassing his normal process and "natural" procedures. The result is not merely wine, but an excellent wine at that. In some ways, what happened in Cana is the exact opposite of what happened fifteen centuries earlier when God was preparing to deliver Israel from the bondage of slavery to the Egyptians. In a sovereign act of supernatural activity, God turned the *entire water supply of Egypt* into blood in an instant of time. He bypassed his normal use of the bodies of humans and/ or animals, of the bone marrow where blood is manufactured from the body's nutrients, and for a single instance in recorded history he made blood directly from water, without using human and/or animal bodies to do so. If God can turn millions of gallons of river water into blood, he can certainly transform a few storage vats totaling about the capacity of a few large aquariums full of water into wine.

1. A SOCIAL FAUX PAS LEADS TO AN UNEXPECTED OPPORTUNITY FOR THE MESSIAH TO ACT (JOHN 2:1-3)

As we look at the incident of the wedding celebration at Cana, it quickly becomes evident that the seventh test question that is being asked of Mary, the mother of Jesus, is "Will you remember who Jesus really is?" We're not told in what capacity Mary was in attendance at the wedding. The narrative set forth in John's Gospel doesn't specify what brought her there. She may have been invited as a guest. John 2:1-2 seems to indicate this:

> *¹On the third day of that week there was a wedding in Cana of Galilee. Jesus' mother was there, ²and Jesus and his disciples had also been invited to the wedding.*

143

The use by John of the Greek verb in verse two indicating that Jesus and his disciples "had also been invited" (Greek: ἐκλήθη δὲ καὶ ὁ Ἰησοῦς καὶ οἱ μαθηταὶ αὐτοῦ, *eklēthē dè kaì ho Iēsous kai hoì mathētaì autou*) is derived from the verb that means "to call" or "to invite" (καλέω, *kaleō*). That Jesus and his disciples had "also" been invited grammatically seems to imply that they were accompanying Mary to the event. As a result, some think this means that Mary was an invited guest, too.

But the verb καλέω (*kaleō*) can also mean "to call," in which case Mary may have attended as part of the catering party, If this is what happened, she would have been a sub-ordinate in attendance to the wedding party's chief caterer, so the nuance of Jesus' and his disciples' attendance at the wedding, whose position of authority (Greek: ἀρχιτρίκλινος, *architrìklinos*) is clearly noted in verse eight. (The word may be translated as "master caterer" or perhaps "master of ceremonies.") So Jesus and his disciples may well have been a last minute invitation to the guest list. As a result, there's a high possibility that adding thirteen or more extra guests to the wedding meant that the celebratory supplies were quickly exhausted. John 2:3 tells us:

> ³*When the wine ran out, Jesus' mother told him, "They don't have any more wine."*

We suggest that this statement by Mary to her son was a politely worded, oblique invitation for help in a socially awkward situation. I've often wondered when perusing this passage whether or not she might have been looking for Jesus to solve a problem that was created by him and his disciples because their presence wasn't expected at the wedding. Or at least, perhaps they drank more of the wine than had been expected. And there's no necessary reason to think that Mary expected a miracle. After all, he hadn't performed one as yet, and his public ministry had just begun that very week.

2. LOVING CORRECTION LEADS TO A REMARKABLE INCIDENT OF DIVINE PROVISION (JOHN 2:4-8)

But the occasion presents an opportunity for Jesus to act, and the result is spectacular. But first he asks a respectful question, followed by the reason for the question. John 2:4-5 explains what happened, and how Mary reacted in faith:

> *⁴"How does that concern us, dear lady?" Jesus asked her.*
> *"My time hasn't come yet."*
> *⁵His mother told the servants, "Do whatever he tells you."*

We invite the reader to keep in mind that Jesus' oblique answer isn't the disrespectful response that it can appear to be in some modern English translations of John's Gospel. As a point of fact, Jesus' address to his mother by calling her "dear lady" is rendered this way by the *Holy Bible: International Standard Version* to communicate the sense of formal respect in light of her obvious position of authority and responsibility at the wedding. Think of a respectful son addressing his mother as he keeps in mind her public exposure and posture at the wedding and you won't be far off the mark.

But then again, there's a hint of a sly suspicion on the part of Mary as Jesus informs her that he didn't intend to come out of the closet, so to speak, as God incarnate by performing a miracle at a wedding. But then again, he acquiesced to his mother's need (and the need of the moment to help the wedding party) and Mary quickly figured out that Jesus had something in mind. Notice how John points out what happened next in John 2:6-8

> *⁶Now standing there were six stone water jars used for the Jewish rites of purification, each one holding from two to three measures. ⁷Jesus told the servants, "Fill the jars with water." So they filled them up to the brim. ⁸Then he told them, "Now draw some out and take it to the man in charge of the banquet." So they did.*

3. A GRATEFUL RESPONSE TO THE WORKS OF THE MESSIAH LEADS TO AN ACKNOWLEDGEMENT THAT GOD SAVES THE BEST TILL LAST (JOHN 2:9-10)

⁹When the man in charge of the banquet tasted the water that had become wine (without knowing where it had come from, though the servants who had drawn the water knew), he called for the bridegroom ¹⁰and told him, "Everyone serves the best wine first, and the cheap kind when people are drunk. But you have kept the best wine until now!"

And so Mary has passed her seventh spiritual challenge. She had raised Jesus as her very human son for about 30 years. But now she has been challenged to see him as more than a good son, a great rabbi, and a wise man. He has supernatural powers that only God can wield. God as the Messiah has used that power to fix a minor social *faux pas*, whereas as we noted earlier, 1,500 years earlier that same God in his pre-Incarnate state had used that same power to demonstrate his power to the household of an unbelieving Egyptian leader and the entire nation he lead so tyrannically.

4. AN APPROPRIATE RESPONSE TO THE PERSON OF THE MESSIAH LEADS TO GREATER TRUST BY MEN AND GREATER GLORY TO GOD (JOHN 2:11)

¹¹Jesus did this, the first of his signs, in Cana of Galilee. He revealed his glory, and his disciples believed in him.

If Mary had not remembered to view Jesus as he really is, the "God with us" promised by the angel Gabriel about 31 years earlier, this opportunity for Jesus to reveal his glory and for his disciples to place their trust in him might not have occurred for many more weeks or even months.

TEST #8: WILL YOU BELIEVE WHAT GOD HAS SAID ABOUT THE MESSIAH?

THE ONE TEST THAT MARY ALMOST FAILED (SORT OF)...

S ooner or later, God will require us to turn our theoretical head knowledge into heart-felt application. It's the nature of life that God wants to turn the purely theoretical into permanent practice. Let's continue our study of the life of Mary the mother of Jesus the Messiah by examining the one test question and challenge that Mary almost failed (at least at first). It's the incident recorded by John Mark in the Gospel of Mark where the faith of Mary is put to the test about whether or not she was going to believe what God had said about her own son.

The Gospel writers Matthew and Luke record the instance, providing separate details not found in Mark's edition of the incident. But only Mark 3:20-22 provides the detail that is the focus of Mary's eighth spiritual test question regarding whether she was going to believe what God had said about the Messiah. Here's how Matthew 12:46-50 records the story without mentioning how Mary reacted to the test:

> *⁴⁶While Jesus was still speaking to the crowds, his mother and brothers stood outside, wanting to speak to him. ⁴⁷Someone told him, "Look! Your mother and your brothers are standing outside, asking to speak to you."*
> *⁴⁸He asked the man who told him, "Who is my mother, and who are my brothers?" ⁴⁹Then pointing with his hand at his disciples, he said, "Here are my mother and my brothers, ⁵⁰because whoever does the will of my Father in heaven is my brother and sister and mother."*

Luke's Gospel also records the incident in Luke 8:19-21:

> *¹⁹His mother and his brothers came to him, but they couldn't get near him because of the crowd. ²⁰Jesus was told, "Your mother and your brothers are standing outside and want to see you."*
> *²¹But he answered those people, "My mother and my brothers are those who hear a message from God and heed it."*

1. AN ADVERSE RESPONSE BY THE MESSIAH'S FAMILY TO HIS POPULARITY (MARK 3:20-21)

Looking at this incident from the standpoint of an observer living 2,000 years after the fact, it may seem difficult for us to understand why Mary responded so adversely to the phenomenal popularity gained by Jesus in such a short time after the start of his public ministry. Mark 3:20-21 gives us the basic facts:

> *²⁰...Such a large crowd gathered again that Jesus and his disciples couldn't even eat. ²¹When his family heard about it, they went to restrain him, because they kept saying, "He's out of his mind!"*

Mark's employment of four specific Greek words in verse 21 of this passage let us know what was going on. These four words are:

- Mark's employment of the Greek word (ἐξῆλθον, *exēlthon*) derived from the verb ἐξέρχομαι (*exérchomai*), which means "to go out" or "to set out" on a specific mission or errand; and,

- Mark's use of the Greek verb (**κρατῆσαι**, *kratēsai*), an infinitive aorist use of the verb **κρατέω** (*kratéō*), which means "to take hold of by force" or "to take custody of"; and,

- Mark's use of the Greek word (ἐξέστη, *exéstē*), which is derived from the verb ἐξίστημι (*exístēmi*), connoting the belief that Mary and her family considered Jesus to be afflicted with some form of unspecified mental, emotional, and/or psychological instability or confusion; and,

- Mark's use of the imperfect verb tense form of the Greek verb "kept saying" (Greek: ἔλεγον, *élegon*), which communicates a sense of continual, repeated complaint that Jesus was out of his mind.

To sum up, what Mark is telling us in this verse is that Mary and her other children specifically left their place or places of residence, intending to take Jesus into some form of protective custodial care in order to keep him from harming himself or others. They thought he was in a state of emotional or mental confusion, and they had come to hold this view of Jesus on a continual, repeated basis.

As we first read this passage, we're prompted to ask how Mary could hold this view of her eldest son, whose very existence she knew to have been conceived apart from any sexual knowledge of a human father, and whose conception had been presented to her more than thirty years earlier.

2. AN ADVERSE RESPONSE BY THE MESSIAH'S ENEMIES TO HIS POWER (MARK 3:22)

But let us say in her defense that there was enormous pressure on her to disparage her own son and his ministry. Take, for example, the adverse response discernible on the part of the enemies of Jesus. A group of professional theologians had been stalking Jesus all over Israel, attempting to interfere with him as he talked to the crowds. Notice how Mark 3:22 sets the stage for us to learn the extent of their animosity:

> *22 The scribes who had come down from Jerusalem kept repeating, "He has Beelzebul," and, "He drives out demons by the ruler of demons."*

If you're looking for a contemporary analogy with which to compare's Mary's situation, think of modern Internet trolls who seem to make it their mission in life to harass people through their weblogs, Twitter feeds, and disparaging op-ed pieces in the media and you won't be far from the truth.

It's hard to imagine Mary and her family remaining unaffected by all of the public slander that Jesus endured from the theological officials of his day. When what seemed to be the entire orthodox theological leadership of first century Israel pronounced Jesus *as being demonic* in nature, origin, and mission, perhaps we shouldn't judge her too harshly for being swayed, at least temporarily, by the prevailing public opinion polls conducted by the theocratic bureaucrats who would later prove deadly in their ability to sway the crowds to reject Jesus at his trial.

This is *especially* true given the high regard in which the theological leadership of Mary's generation were held. Think, if you would for a moment, of the dilemma in which Mary was placed when she listened to her own Jewish leaders and theological experts as they were continually slandering her own son. If you're a Catholic reading this material, try to imagine what dilemma you'd face if one day you heard with your own ears an address from the Pope, the Bishop of Rome, in which the man proclaimed that Jesus of

Nazareth was *demonic* in nature and empowered by Satan himself. Wouldn't that shake up your theological presuppositions?

Put yourself in Mary's place as you think about Mary's eighth test for a moment. And think of the theological leaders of Mary's day who were criticizing Jesus publicly. They weren't just theological leaders. Their behavior had descended into little more than what we'd call today disparaging Internet bloggers and malicious trolls of her day. *Everybody* in both lay and professional theological circles had an opinion, and an astonishingly high number of them were all too eager to tell anybody who would listen why Jesus was doing what he did by the power of Satan himself.

No wonder the lady and her family were confused in the presence of the erroneous theological conclusions of Israel's theological leadership, who should have known better! So let's not be too hard on Mary, the mother of Jesus. As we'll see as we study the last two ten test questions that she was challenged to answer, it's clear from the chain of events that followed that Mary soldiered through the criticism eventually and passed her eighth test.

Then again, it may well be that the public reminder provided to her by Jesus in Mark 3:31-25 served as just the right amount of exhortation she needed in order to make a "mid-course correction" of sorts to her attitude about her son Jesus.

We grant that the theological leadership of first century Israel was a divided lot. On the one hand, you had the liberal Sadducees, who denied the reality of and the ministry of angels. Mary knew by personal experience how false their views were, given that she had met the angel Gabriel face to face more than three decades earlier. The Pharisees were another story. It was about the time of Mary's eighth test that we're studying here that Jesus made clear in no uncertain terms what he thought of the hypocritical Pharisees who turned their traditions into *downright opposition* to the Law of God, so until Jesus' condemnation of the prevailing theological structure of his day became publicly known, it doesn't really surprise us very much that for a season, at least, she was temporarily confused about what God had said about Jesus.

3. A THOUGHTFUL REMINDER BY THE MESSIAH TO HIS FAMILY (MARK 3:31-35)

After Jesus called everyone together, he rebutted and rebuked the Jewish leaders for their unbelief (Mark 3:23-30). Then Jesus addressed the issue of his own family having wavered with respect to their faith in who he was. This took place *after* they arrived on the scene. As Mark 3:31-35 tells us:

> *31 Then his mother and his brothers arrived. Milling around outside, they sent for him, continuously summoning him. 32 A crowd was sitting around him. They told him, "Look! Your mother and your brothers are outside asking for you."*
> *33 He answered them, "Who are my mother and my brothers?"*
> *34 Then looking at the people sitting around him, he said, "Here are my mother and my brothers! 35 Whoever does the will of God is my brother and sister and mother."*

CONCLUSION: WILL WE PASS THE TEST THAT MARY FAILED?

I don't really have a favorite professional sport. But I do like professional baseball. (Having lived in southern California, I've attended my share of games at Anaheim Stadium, where the Los Angeles Angels of Anaheim have their home field.) One of the things I like about professional baseball is that it's a game for those who persevere. I say this because if you've ever studied baseball statistics, if a player has a lifetime batting average of .300, he's considered a world class player. I've been told that any average higher than .250 is also considered excellent.

But consider the reality. A batting average of .300 means that whenever that batter steps into the batter's box, he has a record of *failing 70% of the time.* What other activity is there on planet earth where somebody can fail completely three quarters of the time and *still be considered a world class success!*? So I say baseball is a game for those who persevere.

MARY ALMOST FAILS—AT FIRST

So let's remember that of the ten total test questions that she faced over the span of her life recorded in the New Testament, she passed all of them except for this eighth test, which she almost failed. For a moment, affected by all of the professional theological pundits of her day, she and her family failed to remember what God had told her years before about the son Jesus the Messiah. But later events make it abundantly clear that she stayed the course and remembered what God had said to her about her own son.

Let's also remember that we can learn a valuable lesson from Mary's one single instance of temporary spiritual lapse that is recorded in Scripture. That she obviously recovered from this temporary lapse is seen by her success in dealing with the final two spiritual challenges she faced. Two more difficult challenges lay ahead, just about three years in the future after she came out the other side of her eighth test. Those tests were, *first*, whether or not she was willing to give her dreams about her child into the care of God, and *second*, she would be asked if she were willing to wait on God for his direction for her future life.

And so it is to this final set of two challenges that we turn next.

TEST #9:
WILL YOU GIVE YOUR DREAMS ABOUT YOUR CHILD TO GOD?

HOW WILL YOU RESPOND TO THE DEATH OF YOUR CHILD?

No study of the life of Mary, mother of Jesus the Messiah, would be complete without looking at what was arguably the most difficult of the ten challenges that she faced throughout her life, as we learn from reading the New Testament. The Apostle John tells us about the crucifixion scene in the nineteenth chapter of his Gospel, where we read in John 19:23-27 the following narrative:

> *[23] When the soldiers had crucified Jesus, they took his clothes and divided them into four parts, one for each soldier, and took his cloak as well. The cloak was seamless, woven in one piece from the top down. [24] So they told each other, "Let's not*

tear it. Instead, let's throw dice to see who gets it." This was to
fulfill the Scripture that says,
"They divided my clothes among themselves,
and for my clothing they threw dice."
So that is what the soldiers did.
²⁵Meanwhile, standing near Jesus' cross were his mother,
his mother's sister, Mary the wife of Clopas, and Mary
Magdalene. ²⁶When Jesus saw his mother and the disciple
whom he kept loving standing there, he told his mother,
"Dear lady, here is your son." ²⁷Then he told the disciple,
"Here is your mother." And from that hour the disciple took
her into his own home.

The Appearance of Broken Promises

The day Jesus died must have brought incomprehensible trauma to his mother Mary. Perhaps as Jesus was being handed over to execution as if her son were merely some kind of common criminal, it might have occurred to her to wonder what was to become of the promises that had been made to her by the angel Gabriel on that day more than 34 years before when he said, as the physician Luke recorded in Luke 1:31-33:

> ³¹*Listen! You will become pregnant and give birth to a son,*
> *and you are to name him Jesus. ³²He will be great and will be*
> *called the Son of the Most High, and the Lord God will give*
> *him the throne of his ancestor David. ³³He will rule over the*
> *house of Jacob forever, and his kingdom will never end."*

From the standpoint of human understanding, Gabriel must have appeared to be a false prophet. The afternoon of Jesus' death, *nothing* seemed to be working out as God had promised. The Hope of Israel and of all humanity was to die on a cross.

And so this faithful woman, in whom the fulfillment of all God's work to redeem human beings and to reconcile his Elect to himself would be placed, faces her most difficult test. Bluntly phrased in elegantly simple terms, Mary is being asked whether or not she is willing to give her dreams about her child into the care and custody of God.

WHEN A CHILD PREDECEASES THE PARENT...

By the time Jesus was crucified, his mother Mary would be approaching the age of fifty years. The trauma of watching her eldest son murdered by Roman authorities at the instigation of the theological leaders of Israel surely must have fulfilled in the darkest way the prophetic warning she had heard on the 40th day of Jesus' young life when Simeon had declared to her a prediction that Luke 2:34 indicates was *a blessing from God himself:*

> *34 Then Simeon blessed them and told Mary, his mother,*
> *"This infant is destined to cause many in Israel to fall*
> *and rise. Also, he will be a sign that will be opposed.*
> *35 Indeed, a sword will pierce your own soul, too, so that*
> *the inner thoughts of many people might be revealed."*

As she stood by the cross of Jesus, these words by Simeon may well have been the only prophetic promise concerning her own son that she remembered. After all, he had certainly proved to be a sign that was opposed in Israel. Her soul had been pierced by watching him die a death by the most evil torture that the Roman authorities could devise. And the life and teachings of Jesus had certainly revealed many of the worst of the inner thoughts of friend and foe alike.

WHEN LIFE ISN'T LINEAR

Perhaps it's just a blind presumption on our part today: somehow we think that it's not *natural* that children pass away before their parents. Maybe this assumption is a characteristic of the 21st century culture that pervades our thinking, and maybe it wasn't part of her world view 2,000 years ago. But surely life hadn't turned out for her the way she thought it was supposed to be.

And in this unexpected change of events there came the ninth spiritual test that the New Testament records: Mary is called upon to place the long-term fulfillment of her dreams for her child into the hands of the God who had called her to trust in him more than three decades earlier. If God himself doesn't fulfill his plans for her life, and unless he fulfills those plans *his* way, in *his* timing, and using the means that *he* has ordained, Mary's dreams will never reach the fulfillment for which she longed.

John's Care for Mary

The Apostle John, who wrote the narrative that contains Mary's ninth challenge we're discussing, offered his own long-term support for her, in keeping with the directive given by Jesus that placed her into his long-term care. John writes in John 19:26-27:

> *26When Jesus saw his mother and the disciple whom he kept loving standing there, he told his mother, "Dear lady, here is your son." 27Then he told the disciple, "Here is your mother." And from that hour the disciple took her into his own home.*

Notice, if you would, please, the *humility* displayed by John when he declines to identify himself by name when referring to his own participation in the crucifixion events.

The ancient, first century mode of address to Mary that many English translations of verse 26 render as "Woman" does not contain the brusqueness or curt wording that some modern readers see. In the cultural economy of the first century, the vocative case connoted a polite, respectful, affectionate means of referring to someone who is deserving of the highest and most cordial greeting.

Doubtless, John's unexpected but welcome gesture would have been appreciated by Mary, who apparently Jesus decided should be under John's care rather than under the care of Jesus' other surviving family members.

On The Importance of Having Company when Death Comes to Visit

It seems that Mary was looked after in her ninth spiritual challenge. She didn't have to bear the sorrow of the loss of her son alone. John, the disciple whom Jesus kept on loving, was appointed by God's incarnate son to be the mainstay of her source of human strength and comfort during the immediate aftermath of the crucifixion events.

From that moment on, Mary was taken into John's home for care and company. Christian history and tradition suggests that in later years, she and the Apostle John moved to Ephesus, where she retired. During those retirement years, it would appear that Mary made a significant contribution to the Christian community in that city and was held in high esteem. Many Biblical scholars, including this writer, believe that the Apostle John took a moment from his busy schedule to write her a quick reminder of her duties and responsibilities as a polite hostess for the Christians who lived in her community. That letter survives today as 2 John, the only letter written specifically to a woman in the entire canon of the Old and New Testaments.

MARY PASSED HER NINTH TEST

We conclude our study of Mary's ninth spiritual test question with the rather mundane observation that she passed it. Scripture doesn't tell us about the details of her anguish. We're only told that the Apostle John was appointed by Jesus the Messiah to be a constantly present help in her bereavement.

But then again, her grief only lasted for a weekend.

Sometime on the third day following his death, the son about whom she had received so many awesome promises and prophecies rose from the grave.

The resurrection that Jesus experienced wasn't like the *resuscitations* that had been observed during Jesus' ministry. The people whom Jesus brought back from death were raised to mortal life. They would walk that pathway a second time later on.

Not so with the Son of Man. His return from the tomb was a one-way trip. He is now immortal, and can neither die again, nor be injured or become ill.

Mary's son was restored to life, but he was restored with the proviso that from the date of his resurrection on, he would continue to be about the business of his father, calling out a people for his name's sake, and administering the growth of his Church until the day arrives in the future when he returns to earth, making Jerusalem his international capital city of the entire world, thus taking his rightful throne as the heir to the hegemony of David, just as the angel Gabriel predicted.

Test #10:
Are You Willing to Wait on God to Fulfill His Promises for Your Life?

Christianity is a Waiting Game...

The book of Acts, written by the same author who penned the Gospel of Luke, records one final incident in the life of Mary, mother of Jesus, that we find in the New Testament. For 40 days following his return from the tomb, Jesus visited with his people in various locations surrounding Jerusalem. Given that Jesus had spent the greater part of the weekend following Passover in that tomb, this means that about 43 days following Passover, he was taken to heaven in full view of the disciples.

You can read the narrative in Acts 1:12-14, where the early group of believers gathered during the approximately one week following the Ascension of Jesus the Messiah. Then, on the 50th day after Passover, on the exact day of Pentecost, Luke describes what happened:

> *[12] Then they returned to Jerusalem from the Mount of Olives, which is near Jerusalem, a Sabbath day's journey away. [13] When they came into the city, these men went to the upstairs room where they had been staying: Peter and John, James and Andrew, Philip and Thomas, Bartholomew and Matthew, James the son of Alphaeus and Simon the Zealot, and Judas the son of James. [14] With one mind, all of them kept devoting themselves to prayer, along with the women (including Mary the mother of Jesus) and his brothers.*

The New Testament record seems to record that the period of waiting on God lasted about a week. We say it lasted "about a week" because there is some ambiguity among scholars as to whether or not the 40 days following his death on the cross should be counted from the day of Jesus' death or from the day of his resurrection.

I'm inclined to suggest the 40 days began with his resurrection, which meant only about a week's time lapsed from the date of the Ascension until the commencement of the day of Pentecost.

OUR CALL IS TO WAIT ON GOD AND HIS TIMING

It would be during this seven-day period that Mary, along with every other believer in the resurrected Jesus of Nazareth, were tasked with the spiritual test of waiting on the timing and power of God to begin the next phase of their mission in life, which was to spread the Good News about how Mary's son conquered death, becoming the first fruits of all human beings who have died or will die in the future.

The essence of Mary's final test can be summarized in a single observation: they also serve those who only stand and wait. When God says "Wait!" we are called only to perseverance and patience. He will let us know when it's time to move.

So it was with Mary and with the other 120 people who were gathered in the Upper Room on that Pentecost Sunday. In God's timing, they would be filled with the Spirit of God and become equipped supernaturally to go about the day-to-day missions to which they would be called, to accomplish the mid-range objective of occupying a rebellious world until their Messiah would come again, and in doing so establish his Church, thus working toward accomplishing the long-term goal of glorifying the Son of God by their presence in the world.

CONCLUDING THOUGHTS

HOW WILL YOU ANSWER MARY'S TEN TEST QUESTIONS?

Let's summarize our analysis of what Mary went through in her walk with God, starting with the day she received the angel Gabriel as her guest and listened to what God had in store for her life. Here's a listing of all ten test questions that were put to her over the next three and a half decades or so of her young life, starting from Gabriel's visit and continuing through her teen years until the day of Pentecost following the death of her promised son.

The circumstances of her life as told to us in the narrative of the New Testament Gospels tell us that Mary was asked to respond with an answer to the following test challenges:

- Test #1: Are you willing to trust God with your whole life?

- Test #2: Are you willing to give God your expectations about your life?

- Test #3 Are you willing to walk with God into heartbreak?

- Test #4: Will you give God your illusion of personal security?

- Test #5: Will you give your most important possessions to God?

- Test #6: How will you bear the loss of your spouse?

- Test #7: Will you remember who Jesus really is?

- Test #8: Will you believe what God has said about the Messiah?

- Test #9: Will you give your dreams about your child to God?

- Test #10: Are you willing to wait on God to fulfill his promises for your life?

The overwhelming evidence provided to us by the testimony of the four evangelists Matthew, John Mark, Luke, and John is that she passed all of the test questions that were placed before her except for one (the eighth one), and even in the case of the eighth test, it's clear from the evidence that her lapse was a temporary one.

Given the overall testimony of her life, it comes as no surprise that the early Church held her in such high esteem. While the Protestant community of Christian faith disagrees with some of the legends that have grown up over the centuries, resulting in the Protestant community viewing Roman Catholicism of having an overstated view of her place in the plan of God, nevertheless both Roman Catholic *and* Protestant believers in the Lord Jesus the Messiah may say with one voice that Mary's magnificent poem of praise to God has been abundantly fulfilled throughout the centuries since generations all over the earth have called her blessed.

AFTERWORD:
AN INVITATION TO PARTICIPATE IN A
GRAND ADVENTURE

S ooner or later, all school times end. Academicians call the graduation exercises that take place at the end of class work *commencement* for a good reason: It's because once the lessons have been completed, the time comes for the theoretical to become the practical. Serious life must now begin. Training exercises fade into memories, and the purpose for those lessons becomes manifest.

This book is like those class lessons. Our examination of the ten questions faced by Mary is a theoretical exercise. But for us to allow these studies to remain theoretical exercises only is to waste—perhaps eternally—the opportunity and potential presented to us through those lessons.

In much the same way, the pain and suffering of life should be allowed to bear their proper fruit. And so the necessity of putting the theoretical to work in the realm of the practical brings up the common question asked on so many levels of sincerity by those who are skeptical about the claims of Jesus recorded in the Gospels. The question usually runs something like this:

> *If the claims of Jesus of Nazareth to be God incarnate are true, what proof can you present of the practical reality of God's love being demonstrated through him?*

In essence, the question is "If God exists, prove it." Or better yet, the question is: "So what? How can this possibly matter to *me*?" The answers to questions like these are *anything* but theoretical.

The main thing is this: the Bible makes it clear that everyone will have questions like those articulated above answered with undeniable certainty at the end of days. *Everyone* gets the opportunity to confront God with their objections to life. But there will be surprises. Most notably, most of humanity will discover that the accusers will become the accused. As the New Testament phrases things, we all have an appointment to appear before the judgment seat of the Messiah. As Jesus put it, "All judgment has been given to the Son of Man."

At that time, the stage play we call "real life" will be over, and the Director will come on stage to reward all of the players according to their works. That day will not be the time to choose which side to serve. It will be the time to demonstrate what side has already been chosen.

And so we pose this question: What shall we do when that focus of our deepest hunger and yearnings (or, perhaps, the object of our greatest fears and terrors...) comes undeniably and unavoidably close, enveloped in light unbearable and full of glory, holiness, and righteousness? What shall we do when heaven and earth fly away from the presence of the Lamb? What is to be our response when our greatest fear or our greatest hope invades us and our self-centered tranquility and separateness from all that is truly eternal? In a word, will we be *prepared*? Will we be caught:

- Settled down in our contentment apart from God, or
- Suffering in the miseries created for us by those who have oppressed us, or
- Full of anger because of harvests reaped by us through the consequences of our own unwise choices in life, or
- Faithful and content, having been reconciled to absolute holiness by the one who claimed that he came to redeem his elect

when we come face-to-face with a real-time experience of sovereign holiness, righteousness, and unconquerable power?

Better yet, what will the response be to us from God himself, when he meets us face-to-face at that last day? Will he respond to us as he did to Job, when that long-suffering servant finally had the opportunity to confront God about the troubles which had afflicted him? In Job 38:1-3:

> [1] *The* LORD *responded to Job from the whirlwind and said:*
> [2] *"Who is this who keeps darkening my counsel*
> *without knowing what he's talking about?*
> [3] *Stand up like a man!*
> *I'll ask you some questions,*
> *and you give me some answers!"*

Or shall God respond to us, not with questions such as the above, but with an approving comment? Perhaps as the Master responded to his faithful followers in the parable told by Jesus in Matthew 25:21: "Well done, good and trustworthy servant!"

The importance of preparing for eternity should not be overlooked by the Christian community, either. We Christians address Jesus the Messiah by the term "Lord," but all too often we ignore the implications of how that term should affect our day-to-day responses to life and circumstances. As a famous inscription located on a painting inside the Lübeck Cathedral (German: *Dom zu Lübeck*, or colloquially *Lübecker Dom*) in Lübeck, Germany phrases our obligations to Jesus the Messiah:

> *This Ye Call Me*
> *Ye call Me Eternal, then seek Me not.*
> *Ye call Me Fair, then love Me not.*
> *Ye call Me Gracious, then trust Me not.*
> *Ye call Me Just, then fear Me not.*
> *Ye call Me Life, then choose Me not.*
> *Ye call Me Light, then see Me not.*
> *Ye call Me Lord, then respect Me not.*
> *Ye call Me Master, then obey Me not.*
> *Ye call Me Merciful, then thank Me not.*
> *Ye call Me Mighty, then honor Me not.*
> *Ye call Me Noble, then serve Me not.*
> *Ye call Me Rich, then ask Me not.*

Ye call Me Savior, then praise Me not.
Ye call Me Shepherd, then follow Me not.
Ye call Me Way, then walk with Me not.
Ye call Me Wise, then heed Me not.
Ye call Me Son of God, then worship Me not.
When I condemn you, then blame Me not.

To those who haven't yet met Jesus of Nazareth in his post-resurrection fullness, we ask you this respectful question: Are you looking for proof that God exists, and that he intervenes sovereignly to his greater glory and your great good? If so, you cannot do much better than to invite him to reveal himself to you. To prepare you for this meeting, we invite you to read through the material below, which you can use to begin your journey on what we call the Grand Adventure, and by which you can discover from firsthand experience that when Jesus said "I am the light of the world," he meant *precisely* what he claimed.

HOW TO MEET THE MOST AMAZING MAN WHO EVER LIVED …

If you're ready to meet the most amazing man who ever walked the face of the earth, it's best to begin with the basics. In Matthew 5:3-11, you'll find the basic instructions you need to meet him set forth in remarkable simplicity and succinctness within the opening phrases of the first public statement that Jesus the Messiah made before a large group of people.

STEP 1: ADMIT YOUR SPIRITUAL POVERTY

This is what he told the crowd that had assembled to listen to him:

> *³"How blessed are those who are destitute in spirit,*
> *because the kingdom from heaven belongs to them!*

In making this statement, Jesus of Nazareth informs us that the riches of God's kingdom belong only to the bankrupt in spirit.

The first step to meeting God in the person of Jesus the Messiah is to admit that your own personal positive characteristics have no value when it comes to meeting God's requirements. Human beauty, wealth, wisdom, intellect, abilities, cleverness, and anything else that qualifies us to be a part of the merely human condition are useless criteria by which to define our eligibility to enter the Kingdom of God.

Step 2: Begin to Mourn

If coming to God in the midst of spiritual poverty and bankruptcy is your first step to spiritual redemption, please be advised that taking this first step will immediately take you to your second step: you will begin to experience deep grief.

4 "How blessed are those who mourn,
because it is they who will be comforted!

"The truth will set you free," Jesus once promised his followers, but before it does that, it's going to make you miserable for a short season. God will use your personal poverty of spirit to draw you to himself, and the clearest proof that this drawing process is underway will be that you begin to mourn. You'll grieve over how your behavior and attitudes toward life have offended God and have resulted in endless lost opportunities to enjoy what could have been. Maybe you'll also grieve about those whom you have hurt, betrayed, defrauded, or sinned against.

Step 3: Be Brought to a State of Humility

One of the most immediate results of this mourning will be that it causes you to see your true state before him.

5 "How blessed are those who are humble,
because it is they who will inherit the earth!

You will be made humble, which comes about by beginning to know Jesus the Messiah well enough that you see yourself in perspective. In taking this third step toward salvation you will be made qualified to inherit your place that God made you to enjoy for the rest of eternity.

STEP 4: BEGIN TO HUNGER TO KNOW HIM

After you've realized your own poverty of spirit, after you've begun to mourn because of what has been lost, and after you've begun to see yourself in perspective, compared to his pristine purity and holiness, you will begin to hunger to be like him with respect to righteousness:

> *⁶"How blessed are those who are hungry and thirsty for righteousness,*
> *because it is they who will be satisfied!*

You will begin to want to spend time getting acquainted with God's word, the Bible, because within that book you'll find a road map to personal maturity. You'll seek out the company of like-minded Christian believers, and you'll look for a local church that can encourage you in your new Christian life.

STEP 5: TREAT OTHERS THE WAY JESUS HAS TREATED YOU

God will begin to work deep within you, creating a righteous state before him in which you will take your seat as God continues his work of directing every detail of your life to come. That ongoing process of personal growth will express itself in how you treat others:

> *⁷"How blessed are those who are merciful,*
> *because it is they who will receive mercy!*

You will have been shown mercy, and as a result, you'll begin to show mercy to others after you've realized your own poverty of spirit, after you've begun to mourn because of what has been lost, and after you've begun to see yourself in perspective, compared to his pristine purity and holiness. You will begin to hunger to be like him with respect to righteousness.

STEP 6: LET YOUR HEART BE TRANSFORMED FROM THE INSIDE OUT

As God continues his work deep within you to conform your heart and mind to the image of his son, the Lord Jesus the Messiah, others around you will begin to notice the change you'll have been going through. Some of your friends and acquaintances might even tell you that there's something new about you. Maybe they won't exactly have the words to describe what they see, but see it they will. The truth is, they'll be seeing your purity of heart that has been rooted deep within you:

> [8]*"How blessed are those who are pure in heart,*
> *because it is they who will see God!*

And you'll begin to see God at work, using you to bring a testimony of how God can change the lives of anyone who comes to him, bringing salvation from sin, deliverance from all sorts of bondage, and hope to the hopeless. Jesus the Messiah will have transformed your life, and now you'll see him at work changing others.

STEP 7: LET YOUR LIFE BEGIN TO BE PRODUCTIVE FOR GOD'S GLORY

You will become a peace maker. That is, you'll begin to be known as one who brings peace and security to the lives of those who have neither of these valuable qualities. You'll be given wisdom, whenever you ask for it, to fashion peace out of conflict, serenity out of confrontation, and tranquility out of disruptive relationships.

> [9]*"How blessed are those who make peace,*
> *because it is they who will be called God's children!*

Some of those to whom you minister will begin to tell you that they've finally met one of God's genuine children. "Finally, a true Christian!" could well be what they say about you.

STEP 8: WATCH SOME PEOPLE HATE YOU FOR YOUR NEW LIFE

Be prepared, though, and forewarned: some people will react with animosity, anger, and hatred. The reason for this is that most people are opposed, not only to their own salvation, but to the salvation of others. Not wanting to know God, they won't want you to know him, either, and so you'll find yourself being opposed.

> *[10] "How blessed are those who are persecuted for righteousness' sake, because the kingdom from heaven belongs to them!*

Be prepared for it, because people like this will surely come into your life, and you'll need to learn how to give an answer to these people whom you will find opposing you.

STEP 9: VIEW YOURSELF IN LIGHT OF ETERNITY, NOT PRESENT CIRCUMSTANCES

Keep in mind as you begin your new relationship with God that you aren't the first person who chooses to follow Jesus of Nazareth and then comes into a world of trouble:

> *[11] "How blessed are you whenever people insult you, persecute you, and say all sorts of evil things against you falsely because of me! [12] Rejoice and be extremely glad, because your reward in heaven is great! That's how they persecuted the prophets who came before you."*

HOW TO BEGIN TO RECOGNIZE YOUR OWN POVERTY OF SPIRIT

You have broken God's holy Law. Realizing that this is true is the first step to learning the true state of your standing before God, which is that of spiritual bankruptcy in his perfect, holy, and righteous presence.

You don't think so?

"I'm not so bad," you tell yourself.

Really?

Ask yourself some questions:

- Have you ever lied? Yes, you have. You've broken the ninth commandment.

- Have you ever stolen anything? Yes, you have. You've broken the eighth commandment.

- Have you ever committed adultery? Yes, you have, because Jesus said that to even lust after someone is the same as committing adultery. So you've broken the seventh commandment.

My friend, you have broken three out of ten of God's commandments. And by desiring her or him in the first place, you are coveting someone's wife or daughter, or husband or son. So you've broken the tenth commandment. So far, you've broken four out of ten.

Shall we try for five out of ten? Jesus said to hate someone is to commit the sin of murder in your heart. And that's where sin starts. So you've broken the sixth commandment.

Now let's check the balance sheet: You have admitted that you are a lying, thieving, covetous, murdering, adulterer—and we've only looked at five of the ten.

Shall we go for six? By doing all these things, you have dishonored your father and mother. My friend, you've broken the fifth commandment. Now you've broken six out of the Ten Commandments.

If you will be honest with yourself, you have broken all the others, too. And these are just a summary of God's holy Law.

You've got a problem, my friend.

And it's a serious problem, because the penalty for breaking God's Law is severe indeed. But it's not just your problem. In fact, it's everybody's problem.

The penalty is death, and not just physical death. The penalty is eternal death, separation from God in a place that you really don't want to go to.

But there's some good news. In fact, it's great news. That eternal penalty has already been paid. God Himself paid it and paved the road for our salvation through Jesus the Messiah. Jesus the Messiah is the *only* road, the only means by which we may be saved. Why?

Because his sinless life and his death at Calvary are the perfect substitute for you, satisfying the demands of a holy God.

The road to salvation through Jesus the Messiah is clearly presented in the New Testament. The Apostle Paul's letter to the Romans teaches us some principles about this that will help solve the problem we all face.

1. ALL PEOPLE ARE BORN SINNERS

We are all unrighteous people.

As it is written, "Not even one person is righteous. No one understands. No one searches for God. All have turned away. Together they have become completely worthless." (Romans 3:10-12)

This means that no one is righteous before God and, in fact, no one is even searching for Him.

2. ALL PEOPLE SIN

Our best efforts will never measure up.

… since all have sinned and continue to fall short of God's glory. (Romans 3:23)

This means that *you* have sinned. You have not earned, and do not deserve, eternal life. There are two things you need to know to be saved: *First*, you need to know that you are a sinner who has violated God's laws. *Second*, you need to know that there is a terrible and eternal price for sin.

3. THE PRICE OF SIN IS DEATH

Adam sinned and gave Satan a foothold in the world. By nature, we are all separated from God.

Just as sin entered the world through one man, and death from sin, therefore everyone dies, because everyone has sinned. (Romans 5:12)

We are all born in sin. We deserve death and hell.

4. Jesus Paid Your Debt

He did this by dying in your place.

For the wages of sin is death, but the free gift of God is eternal life in union with the Messiah Jesus our Lord. (Romans 6:23)

5. You Have Earned Death, not Eternal Life

So Jesus, in effect, went to the "Bank of Heaven" and paid your debt for you. Jesus paid the price for you to obtain salvation and eternal life. You cannot earn this payment. Eternal life must be accepted as a free gift from God.

6. Christ Died in Your Place

He paid your price, suffering so that you would not have to suffer eternally.

But God demonstrates his love for us by the fact that the Messiah died for us while we were still sinners. (Romans 5:8)

Due to unconditional love, Christ died in your place, paying a debt He did not owe. We all have an unpaid debt of sin that Christ is willing to pay for us. How do we get our debts paid by Christ? If you accept His payment of your debt by receiving Him as your Lord and Savior, He will make you His child and take you to heaven when you die.

His invitation is open to anyone… even you.

"Everyone who calls on the name of the Lord will be saved." (Romans 10:13)

The word "everyone" includes you. The word "saved" means to be delivered from the guilt and penalty of sin. That includes the present guilt you've incurred. One day in the next life it will include permanent deliverance from the power and presence of it. How do you "call on the name of the Lord" to be saved?

7. You Must Confess your Sin and Declare His Lordship

You declare his Lordship over your life by believing in your heart that God raised Christ from the dead.

If you declare with your mouth that Jesus is Lord, and believe in your heart that God raised him from the dead, you will be saved. For one believes with his heart and is justified, and declares with his mouth and is saved. — Romans 10:9-10

The Bible promises us that God forgives our sin when we accept the work that Christ did for us when He died on Calvary. You can do this by praying this short, simple prayer:

"Lord, Jesus, I have broken God's holy Law. I know that I am a sinner and I need you. I know that you paid the price for my sins by dying on the cross. I ask that you forgive my sins; and I receive you as my Savior and Lord. I thank you for forgiving my sins and giving me eternal life. Take control of the throne of my life. Make me the kind of person you want me to be. Amen."

Look to God's Word for encouragement as you begin your new life in Christ. Remember these simple truths:

- If we make it our habit to confess our sins, he is faithful and righteous to forgive us those sins and cleanse us from all unrighteousness. (1 John 1:9)

- The Spirit himself testifies with our spirit that we are God's children. (Romans 8:16)

- For by such grace you have been saved through faith. This does not come from you; it is the gift of God and not the result of works, lest anyone boast. (Ephesians 2:8)

- For I consider that the sufferings of this present time are not worth comparing to the glory that will be revealed to us. (Romans 8:18)

- I have written these things to you who believe in the name of the Son of God so that you may know that you have eternal life. (1 John 5:13)

- Therefore, if anyone is in Christ, he is a new creation. Old things have disappeared, and—look!—all things have become new! All of this comes from God, who has reconciled us to himself through Christ... (2 Corinthians 5:17-18a)

Be sure to read a portion of God's Word every day and look for a local church to attend so you can be equipped to grow in your new life.

APPENDIX ONE:
DOES ISAIAH 7:14 PROPHESY THAT A *VIRGIN* WOULD CONCEIVE?

BY TIMOTHY W. DUNKIN[1]*

WWW.STUDYTOANSWER.NET

[Editor's note: This material by Mr. Dunkin does not cite The Holy Bible: International Standard Version (ISV). Instead, he cites the Authorized Version, commonly called the King James Version, published on 5 May 1611.]

INTRODUCTION

One of the most maligned verses in the entire Bible is that of Isaiah 7:14. Because this passage is referred to by the Evangelist Matthew as a prophecy which was fulfilled through the conception and birth of Christ, it comes under special assault by Jewish "anti-missionaries" and others who wish to specifically excise the New Testament from its roots and foundation in the Hebrew *Tanakh*. The primary assault made by these individuals centers about the use by Isaiah of the word *almah* in his prophecy.

Whereas *almah* is translated in the KJV as "virgin" and this rendering is supported from the Greek Septuagint translation, Jewish revisers and naturalistic textual critics prefer to render *almah* as "young woman," hoping to undercut the prophetic value of the passage. They claim that if Isaiah were really desiring to prophesy that a virgin would conceive, that he would have used the Hebrew word *bethulah*, which is claimed as a more proper word for "virgin."

---

1 *Mr. Dunkin writes on the Internet using the pseudonym *Titus Quinctius Cincinnatus*. See his web sites at https://meditateinthyprecepts.wordpress.com/ and www.studytoanswer.net.

Contrary to these claims, it is the purpose of this article to demonstrate that *almah* is in fact a more proper term to denote virginity in Hebrew. Further, its translation by early Jewish scholars into the Greek Septuagint demonstrates that the idea of virginity was understood to be conveyed in Isaiah 7:14 and that in pre-Christian Judaism, there was no problem identifying the *almah* of Isaiah 7:14 as being virginal in her conception.

BETHULAH

I will begin by examining the proposed substitute, *bethulah*. Is this word really a more proper word for describing a virgin? In the Hebrew Scriptures, *bethulah* appears 50 times, and its plural *bethuloth* another 10. Out of these 60 uses, though, 14 are figuratively applied to various nations such as Israel, Babylon, Egypt, and so forth, while another 17 are non-committal concerning biological virginity (or the lack thereof), and thus do not directly address the issue at hand (ex. Jeremiah 51:22, "With thee also will I break in pieces man and woman; and with thee will I break in pieces old and young; and with thee will I break in pieces the young man and the maid").

When the remainder are examined more closely, it becomes apparent that the thrust of the word *bethulah* is not biological virginity (either explicitly or implicitly), but rather is the social context of the person(s) which this word represents. The word itself comes from a Biblically unused root meaning "separation, to separate," which would be consistent with a social meaning for this word. As a young woman in an ancient Semitic society, a *bethulah* would indeed have been kept separated from outsiders while under the care of her father, not unlike young women in traditional Middle Eastern cultures such as the Arabs and Berbers today. While the majority of the usage of *bethulah* would connote a young woman who would be virginal due to the social factors involved, this is not always the case. In at least two passages (for a total of three appearances), *bethulah* is used in such a way as to indicate, or at least seemingly suggest, a woman who would not be a virgin according to the biological understanding of that word.

Some clues to the exact meaning of *bethulah* may be gleaned by looking at its use in some of the verses where it seems to be "non-committal" with respect to the issue of biological virginity. In Lamentations 5:11, we see:

They ravished the women [ishshah] in Zion, and the maids [bethulah] in the cities of Judah.

Because *ishshah* is a very general term referring to the female gender, this bit of poetic parallelism can be interpreted as being a synthetic construction in which the "women" in the first line are more particularly addressed in the second line as "maids." Given that *bethulah* has no linguistically direct male counterpart (this being, instead, *bachur*, most often translated as a "young man"), we can surmise easily that a *bethulah* refers in particular to a young person of the female gender, which given the familial system of Israel and other ancient Semitic cultures, would seem to support the notion that *bethulah* is primarily a social term, not one necessarily referring to biological status. Helping to elucidate the distinction of just what a *bethulah* is, we see Ezekiel 9:6:

Slay utterly old and young, both maids [bethulah], and little children [taph], and women [ishshah]...

Thus, a *bethulah* is clearly distinguished both from women, per se, and from little children (*taph*). The word *taph* is most often translated as "little ones" or "little children" in the King James, and nearly always refers to young children and infants, and is often delineated apart from older children (ex. II Chronicles 20:13). The word itself comes from a root (*taphaph*) which means "to trip, to mince," and its derivation in *taph* is attributed by Strong as referring to the "tripping gait of children."[2] Thus, a *bethulah* is not just any young female, but is older than an infant or pre-adolescent child.

In Job 31:1, Job says that he has made a covenant with his eyes, and asks, "...why then should I look upon a maid [*bethulah*]?"

---

2   J. Strong, *Strong's Hebrew Concordance*, entry #2945

Some commentators interpret this as a statement by Job that he would not look upon the wife of another man. Their reasoning is that since the patriarchal society in which Job lived was polygamous, that it would not have been that "out of line" for a man in Job's position to look upon an unmarried girl in desire, as he could simply add her to his harem. However, the testimony of the use of *bethulah* through the rest of scripture would seem to argue against this (though not conclusively, as will be seen with its use in Joel 1:8), and instead be for young, and presumably unmarried, women to be in mind in this passage. Further, the Biblical record of Job pictures him as monogamous, as were most other God-fearing patriarchs in the very early times depicted in the Bible. [3]

The near consistent usage of *bethulah* testifies to its representation of a woman who is not married, and therefore is in the house of her father (or other protector). It is applied to those young women who are specifically shown as still residing in the houses of their fathers (ex. Exodus 22:16, Judges 19:24, etc.) For example:

> *And if a man entice a maid that is not betrothed, and lie with her, he shall surely endow her to be his wife. If her father utterly refuse to give him unto her, he shall pay money according to the dowry of virgins." (Exodus 22:16-17)*

See also such passages as Deuteronomy 22:13-21 and Judges 19:24. The use of *bethulah* is found for women who are specifically stated as not having been married yet:

---

[3]   Remember, Abraham (likely contemporary or nearly so with Job) only had one wife at a time (Sarah, and then Keturah), and his going in to the slave-girl Hagar is generally understood as tacitly disapproved by God because of the lack of faith involved in the act (see Galatians 4:24-25, where Hagar and her child are depicted as types of bondage to the law, distinct from the freedom of faith gained through Isaac, the child of promise). Isaac is also depicted as monogamous with Rebekah, as is Moses with Zipporah. While the societies of the Ancient Near East at the time may have been sometime polygamous (some were, some weren't), this does not necessarily mean that the men who knew God and were not part and parcel with the pagan world-system around them also were. Rather, they can be understood as knowing that God's original plan for marriage was monogamous, and lived accordingly. Jacob, the patriarch with two wives and two concubines, we should note, took a while to get his life really right with God, even though he enjoyed God's mercy throughout. It was during his less-faithful years that he entered into polygyny.

*Neither shall they take for their wives a widow, nor her
that is put away: but they shall take maidens of the seed of
the house of Israel, or a widow that had a priest before.
(Ezekiel 44:22)*

See likewise Psalm 78:63 and Isaiah 62:5. The word is also used of women who reside in the house of their brothers, who act as their protectors.

*And for his sister a virgin, that is nigh unto him, which hath
had no husband; for her may he be defiled. (Leviticus 21:3)*

In these and most other cases where the meaning could be reasonably discernible, *bethulah* would indicate a biological virgin, since in the culture of Israel at the time, for a girl to be under her father's roof meant that she would not have known a man carnally, both because she was not yet married and brought into the house of her husband, and because her father was tasked with protecting her purity until her marriage, and this task was aided by the strict punishments of fornication in the Law. It was considered folly and a shame (and punishable by death) for a girl to play the whore in her father's house. (see Deuteronomy 22:21)

We see evidence for the social context in the story surrounding Tamar and Amnon, in II Samuel 13:1-22. In v. 2, Amnon is said to be "so vexed that he fell sick for his sister Tamar." The reason given for his vexation is that she was a "virgin," a *bethulah*. Now, logically, the biological fact of Tamar's virginity should not be a source of vexation for Amnon. The source of his frustration lay in that she was his half-sister, and thus inaccessible to him according to the Mosaic law (see Leviticus 18:11), yet that she was still "technically" accessible since she was not married off to another man and absent from David's house. She is likely referred to as a *bethulah* in this passage because of the fact that she was still under her father David's roof, it was her place in her father's home, not her biology. After Amnon's crime, Tamar is said to have torn her multi-colored garment with which "virgins were apparelled," symbolizing her status as a favored daughter in the king's house. Afterward,

185

she "remained desolate in her brother Absalom's house"(v. 20). Tamar seems to have lost both her physical virginity and her social place in David's household, likely due to the pressure of Amnon himself, who was then the firstborn and heir to David's throne, and thus favored by his father. At any rate, this history seems to highlight the social overtones of *bethulah*, which usually is contiguous with the biological understanding of virginity.

However, this social context for *bethulah* does not always coincide with biological virginity, at least not as the text always presents the word's use. In Esther chapter 2, the story is told of the search by the Persian king Ahasuerus for a replacement wife for his deposed queen Vashti. He ordered his subordinates to bring to his palace all of the beautiful young virgins of the Empire (Esther 2:2-3). At this point, the "virgins" are referred to as *bethulah*. After the days of the purification of these women, each maiden then came to the king and spent a night with him (vv. 13-14). After this night, these same women are yet still referred to as *bethulah* (vv. 17, 19), even though it is obvious from the context of the passage that they are no longer biological virgins. While this likely argues for application of this word to a non-virgin, it may also be explained through the understanding that the reference to *bethulah* is to their condition before their night with the king, using this literary device to provide a unifying frame of reference, or as a shorthand notation for those "who had been virgins." However, this is less likely than the plain reading of the text itself.

More concretely though, we see in Joel 1:8, "Lament like a virgin girded with sackcloth for the husband of her youth." Here, a woman clearly married is yet referred to with the term *bethulah*. Some commentators interpret this clause as referring to the man to whom this woman was betrothed too (and thus, not formally married to yet) since those betrothed were often referred to as husband and wife. However, the fact that this husband is listed as the "husband of her youth" would seem to argue against this interpretation. Parallel passages which apply in the opposite direction (i.e. to someone's "wife of his youth") clearly indicate in context that the two are already "fully" married, and in fact have been so for some time (see Proverbs 5:18ff, Malachi 2:14ff). Why is this woman referred to as a *bethulah*? Perhaps because she, after the death of her husband, came again under the roof of her father or other close male relative for protection and support, a common feature in ancient cultures of all types (see I Timothy 5:4,16).

Harris, et al. have noted that *bethulah* is not a technical or specific term denoting virginity:

> *Bethulah. virgin, maid, maiden; probably from an unused verb batal 'to separate.' Although Hebrew lexicons and modern translations generally translate bethulah as 'virgin,' G.J. Wenham ("Bethulah"A Girl of Marriageable Age'VT 22: 326-48)* [4] *and Tsevat (TDOT II, p.338-43)* [5] *contest this as a general meaning but prefer "a young (marriageable) maiden." But whereas Wenham does not concede the meaning "virgin" in any text, Tsevat allows this meaning in three out of its fifty-one occurrences (Lev. 21:13f; Deut. 22:19; Ezk. 44:22). In any case, a strong case can be presented that bethulah is not a technical term for virgo intacta in the OT, a conclusion that has important bearing on the meaning of "almah" in Isa. 7:14.* [6]

Another pertinent point when considering the exact meaning of *bethulah* is that, on occasion, the Scriptures deem it necessary to specify the physical virginity of young women referred to by that term. We can see this in the following passages:

> *And they found among the inhabitants of Jabesh-gilead four hundred young virgins, that had known no man by lying with any male: and they brought them into the camp to Shiloh, which is in the land of Canaan. (Judges 21:12)*

> *And the damsel was very fair to look upon, a virgin, neither had any man known her: and she went down to the well, and filled her pitcher, and came up. (Genesis 24:16)*

---

4   G.J. Wenham, "Bethulah, A Girl of Marriageable Age," *Vetus Testamentum* 22, p. 326-348.
5   M. Tsevat, in *Theological Dictionary of the Old Testament*, Eds. H. Botterweck and H. Ringgren, p. 338-343.
6   *Theological Wordbook of the Old Testament*, Eds. R.L. Harris, G.L. Archer, and B.K. Waltke, Vol. 1, Aleph-Mem, p. 137.

It has been remarked upon frequently by commentators that the additional explanation in these cases that a virgin (*bethulah*) had not engaged in sexual activity demonstrates that *bethulah* is not necessarily synonymous with "virgin" in the biological sense. There are some possible objections to this understanding, however. As quoted by Glenn Miller in his article on this subject, Hamilton says:

> *One argument against taking bethulah as virgo intacta is that such an understanding makes the following expression (No man had known her) redundant. But this is not necessarily the case, for the Hebrew Bible provides other instances of redundant or idem per idem constructions. Thus Job 24:21 refers to "the sterile female who does not bear children." One would think that "the sterile female" would be sufficient. Of course sterile women do not bear children. Cf. also Isa. 54:1, "Sing, barren one, who did not bear." Or 2 Sam. 14:5, "I am a widow and my husband is dead." ...A clearer indication that bethulah does not necessarily mean "virgin," as we use that word today, comes from verses like Joel 1:8, in which a bethulah mourns "the husband of her youth." Looking again then at the two phrases in v.16, I suggest that bethulah designates Rebekah as a marriageable woman. The following sentence, "No man had known her" specifies her premarital virginity.*[7]

Miller then goes on to note that the redundancies mentioned by Hamilton as counterpoints are all examples of "hyperbolic, dramatic speech" which use the "piling up" of redundancies for greater emotional effect, and which cannot necessarily be applied to simple narrative such as is relayed in Genesis 24 and Judges 21.[8]

It should also be noted that, at least in Judges 21:12, the virgins are also specifically described as "young" (*naarah*). While described with *bethulah*, they are specified separately as *naarah*, perhaps as

7   V.P. Hamilton, *The New International Commentary on the Old Testament*, The Book of Genesis: Chapters 18-50, Vol. 2, Comment on Genesis 24:16
8   G. Miller, *Response to the Fabulous Prophecies of the Messiah*, Part 2, The Isaiah 7:14 Passage, http://www.christian-thinktank.com/fabprof2.html.

an explanation for why these particular *bethuloth* had not known men in a carnal way, which would argue against *bethulah* being a term specifically addressing biological virginity—it was specified that they were young enough not to have been married before and made *bethulah* by the deaths of their husbands and subsequent return to their fathers' houses.

ALMAH

Seeing that *bethulah* is not a technical term for biological virginity, but rather a social term describing a woman who is separated apart from society (at least symbolically) by being under her father's roof or that of another protector, what then of *almah*? Does *almah* engender a more specific meaning of virginity? The answer to this question is, yes and no.

Almah comes from a root word meaning " to veil from sight, to conceal."[9] *Almah* is notably distinct from *bethulah* on the basis of the fact that it, unlike *bethulah*, has a masculine counterpart based off the same root (while *bethulah*'s counterpart is *bachur*, from a root meaning "to try, to select").[10] This counterpart is *elem*,[11] which also means "something kept out of sight." This is important because, whereas it was noted that *bethulah* is a social term, and that its counterpart *bachur* is also a social term of differing meaning and derivation, *almah* appears to be a "biological" term related to age, nubility, and marriageability, and the root applies across gender.

It is more difficult to build a definite understanding of *almah* due to the much less frequent appearance of this word (7 times) in the Hebrew Scriptures. Its masculine counterpart *elem* appears even less frequently, only three times. The uses of *elem* are pretty standard in referring to a young male child, whether pre-adolescent or adolescent (the word is used to describe the young and victorious David in I Samuel 17:56, where he is called a "stripling" in the KJV).

---

9   Strong, *op. cit.*, entry #5959, from entry #5956.
10   *Ibid.*, entry #970, from entry #977.
11   *Ibid.*, entry #5958.

The usage of *almah*, however, is more interesting and more difficult to discern. The seven verses where *almah* appears are given below:

1. *The singers went before, the players on instruments followed after; among them were the damsels playing with timbrels. (Psalm 68:25)*

2. *And Pharaoh's daughter said to her, Go. And the maid went and called the child's mother. (Exodus 2:8)*

3. *The way of an eagle in the air; the way of a serpent upon the rock; the way of a ship in the midst of the sea; and the way of a man with a maid. (Proverbs 30:19)*

4. *Behold, I stand by the well of water; and it shall come to pass, that when the virgin cometh forth to draw water, and I say to her, Give me, I pray thee, a little water of thy pitcher to drink; (Genesis 24:43)*

5. *Because of the savour of thy good ointments thy name is as ointment poured forth, therefore do the virgins love thee. (Song of Solomon 1:3)*

6. *There are threescore queens, and fourscore concubines, and virgins without number. (Song of Solomon 6:8)*

7. *Therefore the Lord himself shall give you a sign; Behold, a virgin shall conceive, and bear a son, and shall call his name Immanuel. (Isaiah 7:14)*

The majority of these present no problem for the interpretation of virginity. However, Proverbs 30:19 and Song of Solomon 6:8 require treatment at greater depth.

In Proverbs 30:9, the phrase "the way of a man with a maid" is pointed to as an example of the use of *almah* to refer to a non-virginal woman. However, this interpretation is not readily apparent, and is unlikely. Rather, what is discussed in this verse is the blossoming of romantic love in a young man for a young woman, in a process which will eventually finalize in the consummation of their physical relationship in marriage. In covering the gamut of interpretations, Barker *et al.* conclude:

> *What do the ways of an eagle in the sky…a snake on a rock…a ship in the ocean, and a man with a woman have in common? Some writers say the ways of these four are mysterious; others say their ways are non-traceable; others suggest that they each easily master an element that is seemingly difficult. Another suggestion is that they each go where there are no paths. "The way of a man with a maiden" refers to a man's affectionate courting of a woman.*[12]

Further, we see:

> *These verses are another graded (3/4) numerical saying. The understanding of this proverb is not as easy as it appears to be at first sight. Many different solutions have been proposed to explain the wonder occasioned by the four examples. The introductory formula notes that there are four wonderful things in all, with the fourth carrying the main emphasis. These are not objects of investigation, but rather of admiration because they surpass human understanding. The choice of the examples seems to be dictated by what the author felt were truly worthy of wonder. But note that it is not the eagle, serpent, ship, or man that is the real target; it is the "way" (ûrd), repeated in each of the examples. Commentators have proposed various solutions to the "wonder." One is "how"—how does the eagle stay up; how does the serpent move without legs—in other words the mystery of movement. Others have seen something marvelous in that supposedly no trace is left by these objects. This solution resembles superficially the words in Wis 5:10–12, which deals with human transience. That understanding, the absence of any trace, seems to be reflected also in the following v 20. However,*

---

12 *Bible Knowledge Commentary*, Eds. K.L. Barker, E.H. Merrill, and S.D. Toussaint, Vol. 1, Old Testament, Gen. Eds. J.F. Walvoord and R.B. Zuck, comment on Proverbs 30:19.

*one must evaluate better the fourfold repetition of the "way."
The saying underscores the course of an action—that is "the way."
It is not that these objects—eagle, serpent, ship—leave no trace.
Rather, their course is not recoverable. At any given point one
cannot describe the path of the eagle to where it is, or that of
the serpent, or the course of the ship in its traversing the water.
But the way has not been without its goal. If we follow this
lead to contemplating the way of a man with a woman, there
is marvel and astonishment at the course of the attachment that
has made the two one, the mystery of how this was accomplished.
After many encounters and years, they are to become one.
This refers not only to the "yearning" of the woman for the man
(Gen 3:16), or of the man for the woman (Cant 7:10), but to
the whole mystery of their relationship: how it came to be and
what brought them together finally. An observation like this is
singular in the book of Proverbs. One wishes that more of the
numerical sayings would have been handed down. In view
of the not uncommon charge that the sages were simplistic in
their observations and teachings, this openness to wonder and
the contemplation of one of the deepest mysteries in human
relationship is not to be forgotten.*[13]

Delitzsch argues that the fourfold wonders are joined by the
tracelessness of each action described, and that the act of intercourse
(which he notes can leave evidence of itself through pregnancy,
etc.) is not in view but the historical occurrence of the courtship
leading up to the physical relationship.

*That "way of a man with a maid" denotes only the act of
coition, which physiologically differs in nothing from that
of the lower animals, and which in itself, in the externality
of its accomplishment, the poet cannot possibly call something
transcendent. And why did he use the word ba'almah, and not
rather bethulah [with a female] or beishah [id.]? For this reason,*

---

13 *Word Biblical Commentary*, Ed. R.E. Murphy, Vol. 22, Proverbs, comment on Proverbs 30:19.

> *because he meant the act of coition, not as a physiological event,*
> *but as a historical occurrence, as it takes place particularly in*
> *youth as the goal of love, not always reached in the divinely-*
> *appointed way. The point of comparison hence is not the secret*
> *of conception, but the tracelessness of the carnal intercourse.*[14]

What is in view in Proverbs 30:19 is the whole process, traceless and magnificent, of the courtship that occurs between a young man and a young woman, the path of which cannot be followed by an outside observer, the way in which they came together and fell in love that cannot be intimately understood by one not involved. Just as v. 17 contrasts negatively with the three- four combination in vv. 15-16, so also does the adulteress in v. 20 contrast in a negative frame with the way of the man with a maid in v. 19. The adulteress is a parallel counterbalance to the purity and wonder depicted in v. 19, through her impurity and vulgarity.

While this passage offers no definite conclusive support for a specific meaning of "virgin" for *almah*, it likewise provides no firm evidence against it either, on that count it is inconclusive. The weight of exegetical understanding seems, though, to lean towards the notion that the *almah* is virginal, as the understanding is of the courtship that will eventually lead to her marriage and loss of virginity.

The other primary disputed passage is that of Song of Solomon 6:8. Because the "virgins without number" are listed in passage with the queens and the concubines, it is presumed that this indicates that the virgins (*alamoth*) were also women in Solomon's harem, and thus were not biological virgins. This does not seem to be supported by the text, however. This is because the queens, concubines, and virgins are not said to belong to Solomon, or are even associated with him in any sort of personal relationship. In verse 9, immediately after, it says:

> *My dove, my undefiled is but one; she is the only one of her*
> *mother, she is the choice one of her that bare her. The daughters*

---
14   F. Delitzsch, *Commentary on the Old Testament*, Vol. 6, Proverbs, Ecclesiastes, and Song of Solomon, p. 297.

saw her, and blessed her; yea, the queens and the concubines, and they blessed her. (Song of Solomon 6:9)

Now, it is reasonable to suppose that the "daughters" mentioned in this verse are the daughters of Jerusalem, with whom the lovers have had previous conversation (see. Song. Sol. 1:5-8, 2:7, 3:5, 5:8-6:3). Further, it is also not unreasonable to suppose that these "daughters" in verse 9 are a conceptual parallel to the "virgins" in verse 8, especially as both are juxtaposed with the queens and the concubines in much the same manner. As such, there does not seem to be much contextual evidence to suppose that the aforementioned virgins are directly connected with Solomon as they would be if they were part of his harem. This interpretation finds support amongst commentators,

> *The enumeration of the queens, concubines, and maidens [note: Carr uses the NIV], and the contrast with the uniqueness of the beloved (v.9) is usually considered to be a reference to the huge harem of Solomon, none of whose 700 wives and 300 concubines (1 Ki. 11:3) was as attractive to the king as the lady of the Song. The relatively small numbers, sixty and eighty, are supposed by Delitzsch to indicate this episode took place early in Solomon's reign before his harem grew to its fullest number. More probably, no particular harem is being considered. Note the text does not say 'Solomon has' or 'I have', but it is a simple declaration: There are...., and my beloved "is unique" (v. 9 NIV).*[15]

Thus, it is entirely possible that these "queens, concubines, and virgins" are women with whom Solomon has had no formal relations, but are simply women of the city of Jerusalem, both royal and common, against whom Solomon compares his unique and special lover. Criswell[16] also notes that the queens, concubines, and virgins are not said to belong to Solomon, and tenders the argument that they may be royalty which is attending or participating

---

15 G.L. Carr, The Song of Solomon - *An Introduction and Commentary*, Tyndale Old Testament Commentaries, Gen. Ed. D.J. Wiseman, p. 148.
16 W.A. Criswell, *The Criswell Study Bible, KJV*, p. 775, note on Song. Sol. 6:8.

in the marriage procession of Solomon and the Shullamite girl. This argument is supported by Carr, who notes that the particular word for "queens" in this passage (*malkah*) never appears in the Hebrew scriptures in description of the wives of Hebrew kings, but seems to be applied solely the queens of foreign rulers:

> *Queens occurs in the Song only in these two verses, and elsewhere in the Old Testament only of Esther and Vashti (25 times in Esther) and of the Queen of Sheba in I Kings 10 and 2 Chronicles 9. The Aramaic equivalent is used twice in Daniel 5 of the wife of Belshazzar. The word is never used of the wives of Judean or Israelite kings.*[17]

Thus, while this is not completely conclusive that the *alamoth* under discussion are biological virgins, there seems to be no good reason to suppose the alternative. *Almah* can most certainly be understood to refer to physical, not social, condition. Speaking of the Isaiah 7:14 prophecy, Delitzsch says:

> *But it is altogether improbable that the wife of the prophet should be intended. For if it were to her that he referred, he could hardly have expressed himself in a more ambiguous and unintelligible manner; and we cannot see why he should not have said ishtiy or hanviyah, to say nothing of the fact that there is no further allusion made to any son of the prophet of that name, and that a sign of this kind founded upon the prophet's own family affairs would have been of a very precarious nature. And the meaning and use of the word almah are also at variance with this. For whilst bethulah (from bathal, related to badal, to separate, sejungere) signifies a maiden living in seclusion in her parents' house and still a long way from matrimony, almah (from 'alam, related to chalam, and possibly to alam, to be strong, full of vigour, or arrived at the age of puberty) is applied to one fully mature, and approaching the time of her marriage.*[18]

---

17   Carr, *op. cit.*, p. 148.
18   F. Delitzsch, *Commentary on the Old Testament*, Vol. 7, Isaiah, Part 1, p. 217.

Further, it is recognized that *almah* most likely always is referring to one who would be biologically virginal, and that the reliance upon *bethulah* has less foundation than its proponents often portray.

If led by these remarkable coincidences to examine more attentively the terms of the prophecy itself, we find, the mother of the promised child described not as a woman or as any particular woman merely, but as ha'almah a term which has been variously derived from 'lm to conceal, and from alam [Arab.] to grow up, but which, in the six places where it occurs elsewhere, is twice applied to young unmarried females certainly (Gen. xxiv. 43; Exod. ii. 8) and twice most probably (Ps. lxviii. 25; Sol. Song i. 3), while in the two remaining cases (Sol. Song vi. 8; Prov. xxx. 19) this application is at least probable as any other. It would therefore naturally suggest the idea of a virgin, or at least an unmarried woman. It is said, indeed, that if this had been intended, the word bethulah would have been employed; but even that word is not invariably used in its strict sense (see Deut. xxii. 19; Joel i. 8), so that there would still have been room for the same cavils, and perhaps for the assertion that the idea of a virgin could not be expressed except by periphrasis.[19]

This is further supported by *TWOT*:

There is no instance where it can be proved that almah designates a young woman who is not a virgin. The fact of virginity is obvious in Gen, 24:43 where almah is used of one who as being sought as a bride for Isaac. Also obvious is Ex. 2:8. Song 6:8 refers to three types of women, two of whom are called queens and concubines. It could be only reasonable to understand the name of the third group, for which the plural of almah is used, as meaning "virgins." In Ugaritic the word is used in poetic parallel with the cognate of bethulah.[20]

---

19   J.A. Alexander, *Commentary on the Prophecies of Isaiah*, pp. 167-8.

20   *Theological Wordbook of the Old Testament*, Eds. R.L. Harris, G.L. Archer, and B.K. Waltke, Vol. 2, Nun-Taw, p. 672.

Motyer additionally comments:

The translation virgin (almah) is widely disputed on the ground that the word means only "young woman" and that the technical word for "virgin" is bethulah. Of the nine occurrences of alma those in 1 Chronicles 15:20 and the title of Psalm 46 are presumably a musical direction but no longer understood. In Psalm 68:25; Proverbs 30:19 and Song of Solomon 1:3 the context throws no decisive light on the meaning of the word. In Genesis 24:43 and Exodus 2:8 the reference is unquestionably to an unmarried girl, and in Song of Solomon 6:8 the alamoth contrasted with queens and concubines, are unmarried and virgin. Thus, wherever the context allows a judgment, alma is not a general term meaning "young woman" but a specific one meaning "virgin". It is worth noting that outside the Bible, so far as may be ascertained, alma was never used of a married woman.[21]

Unger's conclusion about Isaiah 7:14 is that *almah* was used because it most properly combines the understanding of both virginity and marriageable age (the latter being a meaning which is much less obvious in *bethulah*). Concerning *almah*, he notes:

Although the primary idea of this word is not unspotted virginity, for which the Hebrews had a special word, bethulah, "virgin" is, nevertheless, the proper rendering in Isaiah 7:14 of almah, which may not only take this meaning (Gen. 24:43), but in light of Matt. 1:23 must take this meaning. The Holy Spirit through Isaiah did not use bethulah, because both the ideas of virginity and marriageable age had to be combined in one word to meet the immediate historical situation and the prophetic aspect centering in a virgin-borne Messiah.[22]

And while we have seen that Unger's statement about *bethulah* being a special word for unspotted virginity is incorrect,

---

21 J.A. Motyer, *The Prophecy of Isaiah: An Introduction and Commentary*, comment on Isaiah 7:14.
22 *Unger's Bible Dictionary*, Ed. M.F. Unger, "Virgin," p. 1159.

he nevertheless puts forth a strong argument concerning the particular use of *almah* in Isaiah 7:14.

To conclude this section, we can reasonably state that both *bethulah* and *almah*, given the social and moral structure of theocratic Israel, would implicitly contain the meaning of "biological virginity," excluding the figurative and personifying uses of *bethulah*. Both words can be considered to be roughly synonymous, though not completely so. Also, neither are words which specifically mean "virgin." However, there are differences in the implications of these words, and *bethulah* appears to be a word engendering social meanings of separation and protection under the father or other protector's roof, while *almah* seems to imply physical characteristics of youth, nubility, and readiness for marriage. Also, while *bethulah* shows some evidence of being used in reference to women who definitely would not be virginal, the same cannot be reasonably said for *almah* and thus, *almah* would appear to be a more technical word to convey the idea of virginity, and its use in Isaiah 7:14 would be more appropriate, both contextually and prophetically, than that of the alternative *bethulah*.

EVIDENCE FROM COGNATE SEMITIC LANGUAGES

To gain a greater understanding of the finer meaning of *almah* and *bethulah*, we may also turn to the concurrent illustration provided by the use of their cognates in other ancient Semitic languages. In doing this, we see that the information provided by cognate Ancient Near Eastern languages concerning both of these words tends to give support to the conclusions drawn above from the Hebrew of the Old Testament.

In these cognates, the *btlt* or similar root (analogous to *bethulah*) often describes women who exist in the social condition of being under the lordship of their father, husband, or other *ba'al* (a word meaning "lord" which is often used to describe a husband in ancient Semitic texts, both Biblical and secular). As such, it becomes immediately obvious that *btlt* cannot be considered as a descriptor for biological virginity. The most widely known and obvious example of this is found in the ancient Ugaritic mythological texts, Ugarit being a Canaanite city closely allied philologically to lower Canaan and Phoenicia. In Ugaritic and other Canaanite mythology, the goddess Anat (or Anath) is consistently referred to as *btlt 'nt*, the Virgin Anat.[23] This is despite her quite apparent sexual activity and pregnancy. Cassuto demonstrates some confusion on this point when he states:

> *A customary epithet applied to her [Anat] in Ugaritic writings is btlt ("the virgin"), and it is impossible to tell whether the Canaanites understood this title literally, or whether they attributed to it a symbolic connotation only.*[24]

However, from the available evidence about Anat, the literal interpretation of "virgin" as *virgo intacta* would not likely have been reasonably held by the Canaanites, and that her title "Virgin" was some sort of sacramental designation would seem to make more sense. In this mythological system, Anat is depicted as marrying her brother Baal after she rescues him from his imprisonment in the underworld.[25] Canaanite legend from the Ras Shamra tablets further depicted Anat, in the form of a cow, being impregnated by Baal after his restoration, and giving birth to a wild ox.[26] Canaanite iconography even depicted sexual intercourse between Baal and Anat. In further mythology transferred to the Semites (such as the Aramaeans) from the Canaanites, Anat was presented as the consort of Baal-Hadad, a Semitic storm and fertility god.[27]

Thus, in Canaanite at least, *btlt* does not seem to present itself as denoting biological virginity. In other cognate Semitic languages, as well, we see that *bethulah* does not specifically denote virginity.

---

23 J. Gibson, *Canaanite Myths and Legends*, pp.45, 56, etc., Ed. G.R. Driver

24 U. Cassuto, *The Goddess Anath*, p. 64.

25 A. Baring and J. Cashford, *The Myth of the Goddess: Evolution of an Image*, p.457.

26 See R. Patai, *The Hebrew Goddess*, p.61.

27 M. Eliade, *Patterns in Comparative Religion*, p. 90.

> *The Akkadian cognate, batultu denotes "primarily an age group: only in specific contexts...does it assume the connotation virgin" (CAD II: 174).*[28] *J.J. Finkelstein ('Sex Offences in Sumerian Laws,' JAOS 86:355:72)*[29] *and B. Landsberger 'Jungfräulichkeit: Ein Beitrag zum Thema Beilager und Eheschliessung' in Symbolae juridicae...M. David....edid. J.A. Ankum..., II (Leiden, 1968, pp. 41-105) have underscored in independent studies that the word is normally best understood as "young (unmarried) girl." In fact, there is no one word for "virgin" in Sumerian or Akkadian; that concept is expressed negatively by "who is not deflowered."*

So also, "In Ugaritic *btlt* is a frequent epithet for Anat, Baal's wife, who repeatedly has sexual intercourse (cf. A. van Selms, *Marriage and Family Life in Ugaritic Literature*, London, 1954, pp. 69, 109).

In a Shiite tradition, Fatima, though the mother of Hasan and Hussein along with other children, bears the title *batul* (C. Virolleaud, *Le Theatre Persan*, Paris, 1950, p. 37). And in an Aramaic text from Nippur, Montgomery interprets the phrase, *btwlt* "travailing and not bearing," to denote a hapless wife suffering from miscarriages and other female complaints (*Aramaic Incantation Texts from Nippur*, Philadelphia, 1913, p.131).

Tsevat concluded that the word "does not mean *virgin* in any language exclusively (Aram.), mainly (Heb.), or generally (Akk . [and Ugar.?])."(p. 340)[30,31]

Harris, et al. also note that the ancient Egyptian (not strictly a cognate) parallel for *bethulah* (*hwn.t*), may denote a young, marriageable girl who has or has not had sexual relations. Further, they reveal that this term is used to describe both the king's protectors in the Pyramid texts, explicitly called his mother, and also the goddess Isis who in a sarcophagal oracle is said to have become mysteriously pregnant.[32] They quote Tsevat as concluding:

28 *The Assyrian Dictionary*, Eds. I.J. Gelb, et. al., Vol. 2, p. 174.
29 *Journal of the American Oriental Society*, Vol. 86, series 355, p. 72.
30 M. Tsevat, in *Theological Dictionary of the Old Testament*, Eds. H. Botterweck and H. Ringgren, p. 340
31 *Theological Wordbook of the Old Testament*, Vol. I, p. 137-138.
32 *Theological Wordbook of the Old Testament*, Vol. 1, p. 137.

> *It can be stated that hwn.t is not used to denote biological virginity, but rather youthful vigour and potential motherhood.*[33]

Thus, the notion that *bethulah* or its cognates would present a more "proper" or "representative" word for "virgin" is not supported by the data from cognates and Egyptian, another important ancient Near East language.

What about *almah*? We find that, much like in Hebrew, this word in cognate languages depicted a woman who would be quite similar to a *bethulah* in most respects, but yet who could more properly be considered as a biological virgin. Looking again to the evidence of Canaanite mythology, we see *gmlt* (the *almah* cognate) used to describe the girl Huray, sought for marriage by the god Keret, and who is described as an unwedded, virginal lass.[34]

Likewise, we find in Arabic a piece of information concerning *almah*. In the Qur'an, a near-textbook example of early standard Arabic and little changed from antecedent Northern Arabian dialects (Thamudic, Saifitic, etc.), we find *almah* presented as representing biological virgins. In Surah 56:36, we find (transliterated), *FajaAAalnahunna abkaran*, which is variously translated as "And made them virgins" (Pickthall translation) and "And made them virgins - pure (and undefiled)" (Yusuf Ali translation). This usage reflects the sometime tendency in Arabic to render an "n" for what appears as an "m" in other Northern Semitic languages, such as when the pluralization of masculine Hebrew nouns with *-im* appears as *-yyin* in Arabic. The context of this passage is the Quranic description of Paradise, and the virgins under discussion are the perpetual virgins who will accompany the righteous for eternity in the Quranic mythology, so remarked upon by Western commentators. Both Muslim and Western Orientalist commentary on this passage has consistently understood these women to be biological virgins, even to the point that they can "regenerate" their virginity perpetually.[35]

---

33 Tsevat, *op. cit.*, p. 339.

34 Gibson, *op. cit.*, p. 87.

35 See e.g. E.M Wherry, *Commentary on the Qur'an*, Vol. 4, p. 111, note on Surah 5:35; S.A. Ali, *Qur'an The Fundamental Law of Human Life*, Vol. 14, p. 158; M.A.M. Daryabadi, *Tafsir-ul-Qur'an: Translation and Commentary of the Holy Qur'an*, Vol. 4, p. 301, note #374.

Hence, *almah* as it appears in Semitic cognates seems to evince a much stronger tendency towards denoting biological virginity than does *bethulah*. This, in turn, would strike another blow to the arguments against the use by Isaiah of *almah* in Isaiah 7:14.

A WORD ABOUT *PARTHENOS* - ITS MEANING AND USE

We now turn to the use of the Greek word of interest in our discussion - *parthenos*. *Parthenos* is important both because it is the term which is used in Matthew's interpretation of the Isaiah 7:14 prophecy, and also because it is this word which is found in the Greek translation of the Old Testament, the Septuagint, at that verse.

Through examination of the use of *parthenos* in secular Greek literature from across a range of time periods, it seems that this word is nigh well synonymous with both *almah* and *bethulah*, which is to be expected when we consider that in the Septuagint, the translators rendered both of these Hebrew terms as *parthenos* in the Greek. However, when we consider the differentiation earlier seen between *bethulah* and *almah*, we see that *parthenos* appears to be much more compatible with *almah* where the issue of biological virginity is concerned.

Parthenos, like *almah*, seems to be a word which refers to a young, marriageable woman, but somewhat more strongly implies the pre-sexual nature of the maiden. Euripides (480-406 BC), in *Iphigenia in Aulis*, describes a "maiden's marriage" using the term *parthenois*, and the context is that of a previously unmarried and chaste young woman.[36] In line 738 of the same, reference is made to *parthenosi*, a maiden's apartment in which the unmarried daughter is sequestered away, and in line 731, the term *parthenous* is translated as "unmarried daughters." Strabo (63 BC-24 AD) states:

> *Or as the unwedded virgin (parthenos) who, dwelling on the holy Didyman hills, in the Dotian Plain, in front of Amyrus, bathed her foot in Lake Boebeïs...*[37]

---

36 Euripides, *Iphigenia in Aulis*, lines 718, 740.
37 Strabo, *Geography*, Bk. 14, Chap. 1.40.

Plutarch (45-125 AD) further emphasizes both the youth and marriageability of this sort of young woman when he writes:

And if he discovers a young man in the house of a rich and elderly woman, waxing fat, like a cockpartridge, in her service, he will remove him and give him to some marriageable maid (parthenon numphên) that wants a husband. Thus much, then, on this head.[38]

Usage, however, indicates that the term is not applied to any and all young women who are unmarried, but those specifically who are at the age and ready to enter into marriage. Plato (427-327 BC) shows a distinction between very young girls and young women, where he says:

As to women,--it is not worthwhile to make compulsory laws and rules about their taking part in such sports; but if, as a result of earlier training which has grown into a habit, their nature allows, and does not forbid, girls [paidas] or maidens [parthenous] to take part, let them do so without blame.[39]

The word is often used to describe a young woman who is still under the care and protection of her father or other protector, demonstrating a *bethulah*-like "social" application of the word. Xenophon (c. 430-355 BC) also uses *parthenous* to describe girls under the care of the father's household.[40] In Sophocles' (496-406 BC) *Oedipus Tyrannus*, the two daughters of Oedipus, Ismene and Antigone, are referred to as,

My two girls [parthenoin - fem. gen. dual], poor hapless ones--who never knew my table spread separately, or lacked their father's presence, but always had a share of all that reached my hands.[41]

---

38 Plutarch, *Lives*, Solon, Chap. 20.1.
39 Plato, *Laws*, Sect. 843d.
40 Xenophon, *Memorabilia*, Bk. 1, Chap. 5.2.
41 Sophocles, *Oedipus Tyrannus*, line 1462.

However, the father need not be the only protector, as a couple of passages from Pausanias (early 2nd c. AD) indicate. For instance, he describes Callirhoe as a "maiden" (*parthenou*), and mentions that she lives with foster parents.[42] Also, he uses *parthenos* to describe a young, fatherless girl living with her mother, indicating that she is unmarried and under the care of her surviving parent.[43]

Parthenos is used to describe one who is specifically stated to be completely chaste. Further, this word is often used to describe those who were unquestionably biological virgins. In Greek mythology, two goddesses stand out as idealized examples of sexual chastity - Athena and Artemis. Both are frequently given the epithet of "virgin," but unlike the Canaanite myths discussed earlier, there is no hint that either of these goddesses were ever considered to be sexually active, either licitly or illicitly. Athena, who was both unmarried and sexually chaste, was universally considered to be a virgin and was described as such:

> *Meanwhile we sing of how the son of Amphitryon, a bold-minded man, left Oechalia devoured by fire, and arrived at the headland with waves all around it; there he was going to sacrifice from his booty nine loud-bellowing bulls for Cenaean Zeus, lord of the wide-spread clouds, and two for the god who rouses the sea and subdues the earth, and a high-horned unyoked ox for the virgin Athena, whose eyes flash with might. Then a god, useless to fight against, wove for Deianeira, to her great sorrow...*[44]

Further, in the *Homeric Hymns* (anonymous, most composed about the 7th c. BC), Athena is referred to as a "pure virgin" (*parthenon aidoien* - literally, holding herself a virgin) as a mark of her chastity.[45] Apollodorus (c. 150 BC) describes Athena also as a "chaste virgin" (*parthenos*) who defies the attempt by Hephaestus to rape her.[46]

---

42 Pausanias, *Description of Greece*, Bk. 7, Chap. 21.3.
43 *Ibid.*, Bk. 4, Chap. 19.1-5.
44 Bacchylides, *Odes*, Poem 16, line 17 (Bacchylides lived c. 520-450 BC).
45 *The Homeric Hymns and Homerica*, Trans. H.G. Evelyn-White, Chap. 28.5.
46 Apollodorus, *Library and Epitome*, Book 3, Chap. 14.12.

Artemis also was famous for her complete chastity and virginity. Strabo[47] uses the term to describe girls (*parthenous*) who are said to be "ripe for marriage," and certain maidens (*parthenous*) who were coming to sacrifice at the Temple of Artemis at Limnae. These maidens were part of the cult of Artemis, who was in classical mythology strongly attached to her virginity, meaning physical chastity, even to the point of killing a man who accidentally saw her unclothed.[48] Pausanias also describes the priestess of the temple of Artemis at Aegeira using the term *parthenos*, saying she remains priestess until she marries.[49] Diodorus Siculus (90-21 BC) speaks of the ancient custom of having virgins (*parthenous*) deliver the oracles of Artemis because "They are like Artemis is," and "Their natural innocence is intact," referring to the biological aspect of their virginity.[50]

Pindar (522-443 BC) even refers to a virgin conception, that of Perseus, the son of Danae, who was spontaneously impregnated by a fog of gold (which some sources say was from Zeus). She is called "the virgin [*parthenos*] goddess," and she had actually been shut up in a locked room by her guardian to keep her away from the amorous advances of men.[51]

The goddesses were not the only ones described by this word in reference to obvious physical virginity. Demosthenes (384-322 BC) discusses the Attic law that stated concerning the elected king "that he should marry a virgin (*parthenon*) who had never known another man."[46]

As with the cases of redundancy with *bethulah*, this demonstrates that *parthenos* is not a technical term for biological virginity, but carries social overtones which need to have the physical aspect specified where necessary.

However, unlike *bethulah*, there do not seem to be any instances in which *parthenos* is used to describe a woman who would, or could, be logically considered as sexually active. In describing

---

47 Strabo, *op. cit.*, Book 6, Chap. 1.8.
48 Ovid, *Metamorphoses*, Book 3, lines 138-249, the story of Actaeon is related here..
49 Pausanias, *op. cit.*, Bk. 7, Chap. 26.5.
50 Diodorus Siculus, *Library*, Book 16, Chap. 26.6.
51 Pindar, *Pythian Odes*, Poem 12, line 18.

married women, the term *gune* is employed, which is a word that properly refers to mature women, ones who in that society would be expected to be married. For instance, Aristotle (384-322 BC, whose extant works use *parthenos* twice, once in a way which is neutral for this discussion, but the other which is quite certain), records a portion of an iambic from Anaxandrides lamenting girls who are slow to marry, which includes "My daughters (*parthenoi*) are 'past the time' of marriage..."[47] Thus, his daughters are old enough that they are expected to have been married by that time, yet were not, and are still referred as *parthenoi*, showing that *gune* is not really a general term for women of a certain age group, but that it seems to more specially refer to those in the social condition of marriage. Xenophon also draws a distinction between "women" (*gunaixi*) and "maidens" (*parthenois*) when he urges the Greeks to avoid the pleasures of Persian women and other luxuries and to return to Greece.[48]

Thus, as with *almah*, *parthenos* is a word which, while not always specifically referring to the biological meaning of "virgin," in practice would carry that connotation throughout, and is often specifically employed in that capacity. Further, it does not demonstrate use which would suggest a non-virginal woman, and thus can be understood to be a good "technical" word for "virgin" as well.

HELLENISTIC JEWISH USE OF *PARTHENOS* - AN EXAMPLE

Before delving into the Septuagintal use of *parthenos* in Isaiah 7:14, a look at the use by another Jewish source is in order. Josephus (1st c. AD), who lived roughly two and a half centuries after the translation of Isaiah into Greek for the Septuagint, provides us with a picture of *parthenos* which accords well with the other Greek use seen above. Josephus' testimony, though, is important because he wrote in the Christian era, and thus demonstrates what a perhaps typical Jewish conception of *parthenos* was, even after Christians began to use Isaiah 7:14 to point to prophetic fulfillment through Christ.

Josephus relates the Biblical story of Abishag, who served as a bedmate for King David:

> *David was now in years, and his body, by length of time, was become cold, and benumbed, insomuch that he could get no heat by covering himself with many clothes; and when the physicians came together, they agreed to this advice, that a beautiful virgin, chosen out of the whole country, should sleep by the king's side, and that this damsel would communicate heat to him, and be a remedy against his numbness. Now there was found in the city one woman, of a superior beauty to all other women, (her name was Abishag,) who, sleeping with the king, did no more than communicate warmth to him, for he was so old that he could not know her as a husband knows his wife. But of this woman we shall speak more presently."* [52]

Abishag is referred to as a *parthenos*, and was not "known" by King David due to his age and inability. Given the lesson which he learned from the episode with Bathsheba, it is unlikely that Abishag would have been a married woman (given the bad testimony it would engender), nor is she described as a widow, which would be very odd if she were one.

Josephus refers to Rebekah as a virgin, [53] just as the OT uses for both *bethulah* and *almah*, where he records that she says that Laban is the "guardian of her virginity" (*parthenias*).

Josephus also uses the term *parthenos* to refer to a virgin being conducted out with her bridegroom to her wedding, [54] and describes Tamar in David's house (thus before her rape) as "yet a virgin," [55] which is important because of what was taken from her when Amnon raped her. Afterwards, she had to remain desolate in Absalom's house after this, unable to marry (II Samuel 13:20). Thus, we see that Josephus specifically notes that she was "yet a virgin" before she was forced by Amnon, which would seem to imply that Josephus viewed *parthenos* as having specific physical overtones.

---

[52] Flavius Josephus, *Antiquity of the Jews*, Bk 7, Sect. 343-4.
[53] *Ibid.*, Bk 1, Sect. 248.
[54] *Ibid.*, Bk 13, Sect. 20.
[55] *Ibid.*, Bk 7, Sect. 162

Josephus also[56] delineates virgins (*parthenous*) apart from women who have been married before or who are harlots. She is, he cites, to be "of good parents" (who would protect the chastity of their young daughter). Further, in sec. 246, Josephus covers the case of the man who is espoused to a virgin and "afterward" finds her not to be one. If she is found guilty, she is killed because she did not maintain her virginity (*parthenias*) until she was "lawfully" married, which could indicate either an elopement or fornication – either way, the emphasis seems to be clear as to the state of her virgin-borne parts, not whether she was pregnant. I say this because some commentators argue that the "tokens of virginity" required (see Deuteronomy 22:17, 20) are evidences of the young girl's menstruation, not to the sheet of the wedding night. While there are good arguments for this case,[57] I would also note that there are problems which could present themselves with that interpretation. If her loss of virginity had occurred within a mere matter of days before her groom found out about it, she may not have reached her next period of menstruation anywise, and thus could elude the command of God on this matter through this "loophole." A more "foolproof" way of determining her virginity would seem to be the outcome of the *de facto* determination made on the wedding night.

At any rate, Josephus' use of *parthenos* does not seem to differ in any substantive degree from that of Greek and Hellenistic writers all across the ages of Greek literature.

THE TRANSLATION OF ISAIAH 7:14 IN THE SEPTUAGINT

Let us now turn to the use of *parthenos* in the Greek rendering of Isaiah 7:14 in the Septuagint. The Septuagint provides for us probably the most neutral, non-sectarian glimpse of how pre-Christian Hellenistic Jews interpreted Isaiah 7:14. This verse, of course, renders *almah* as *parthenos* in the Greek. It is important to note that the Septuagint translators were Hebrews of the Hebrews, well-educated and respected Jewish rabbis. It is also important to note

---

56 *Ibid.*, Bk 4, Sect. 244ff.
57 See *Theological Wordbook of the Old Testament*, Vol. 1, p. 138.

that the translation work on the Septuagint was completed nearly two centuries prior to the Christian era. Unlike the calumniations against Matthew's use of the word *parthenos* to describe Mary, it is patently impossible for one to make the charge of "Christian interpolation" against the appearance of *parthenos* in the Septuagint Isaiah 7:14.

Unlike later Jewish and Judaizing revisers of the Septuagint in the Christian era, such as Aquila and Symmachus, both of whom retranslated the verse using *neanis* for sectarian purposes, the original Septuagint translators had no reason to bias their translation, and thus their use of *parthenos* can be considered most authentic, and it is fairly obvious that they were interpreting Isaiah 7:14 to be referring to an unmarried (and therefore either specifically or implicitly virginal) young woman, for this is what the record of Greek usage of *parthenos* from before, at, and after their time would suggest. This would seem to argue against modern Jewish arguments that the verse is (or was) understood to be referring to either Ahaz's or Isaiah's wife conceiving and bearing a child, as *parthenos* is not used in this sense in Greek. If this were the understanding, the translators would likely have used *gune* to describe the woman in Isaiah 7:14.

Throughout the Septuagint, the general word used to translate both *almah* and *bethulah* is *parthenos*, though *neanis* is used to render *almah* in both of that word's appearances in the Song of Solomon. Interestingly, the most explicit place in the Hebrew Old Testament where *bethulah* is used to denote a woman who is obviously not a virgin is translated as *numphos* (young), not as *parthenos*, in Joel 1:8.

SUMMARY AND CONCLUSIONS

From the study above, it should be clear to the reader that the traditional view of the conception of Jesus Christ as a fulfillment of prophecy given in Isaiah 7:14 is the correct assessment. Despite arguments to the contrary, *almah*, used in that verse, indeed appears to be a better technical term to describe a biological virgin than is *bethulah*, even though neither carry that specific connotation.

The appearance of *parthenos* in the Gospel of Matthew with respect to the fulfillment of Isaiah 7:14 and the interpretation of this as speaking of a physically virginal girl, both also appear to be correct, and in fact rest on prior Jewish interpretation as found in the Greek Septuagint translation which was the initial Jewish Old Testament in Greek. Thus, while Jewish "anti-missionaries" and a host of others may wish to assail the accuracy, propheticity, and veracity of the Bible, they would be wrong to make their attempts with this prophecy. Though the fulfillment of Isaiah 7:14 forms only one, small facet of the testimony to Christ's Messianicity, it is a brick in the foundation in which Christians can put their full and complete trust.

APPENDIX TWO:
A COMMENTARY ON 2 JOHN

BY CHARLES W. MISSLER, PHD
KOINONIA INSTITUTE
REPOROA, NEW ZEALAND

INTRODUCTION

The early Church in the first century was under attack from both the inside and the outside. Sounds like today. It should not surprise us that the Holy Spirit has anticipated every conceivable form of attack and diversion, and John's three letters are full of insights that are timely for each of us at the personal level as well as the corporate level.

PURPOSE OF JOHN'S MINISTRY

30 Jesus performed many other signs in the presence of his disciples that are not recorded in this book. 31 But these have been recorded so that you may believe that Jesus is the Messiah, the Son of God, and so that through believing you may have life in his name. (John 20:30-31)

THE APOSTLE JOHN

The author of this letter is the apostle John, who was the brother of James (James the Greater, as he is sometimes called). And John was probably the younger son of Zebedee and Salome, born in Bethsaida. His father was apparently a man of some wealth, as John was trained in the typical education of Jewish youth, and he ended up becoming a part of the fishing business that the sons of the Zebedee had, and also Peter and Andrew. They were his partners together—or competitors, it's not clear—but in any case, they were all part of the fishing industry there.

John was part of Jesus' intimate insider circle. There were seventy, and of the seventy there were twelve. And of the twelve there were three. And he was part of that group of three: Peter, James and John. They were there when Jairus' daughter was raised from the dead in Matthew 9, as well as the Transfiguration of Jesus in Matthew 17. The three of them enjoyed a closer proximity at Gethsemane, as highlighted in Matthew 26. They along with Peter's brother Andrew were also at the Olivet Discourse.

John calls himself "the disciple whom Jesus loved"; he never uses his own name in his narrative. And that last week of Jesus's earthly ministry, he followed with Peter—everyone else had split— but the two of them hung in close to see what was going on. John had access to the council chamber at the trial, which means he had some kind of leverage. He was also there at the foot of the cross. Mary was assigned to his care as Jesus hung on the cross, which is strange when you think about it, because Jesus had four brothers. Yet, Jesus consigned His mother, Mary, to John, not one of His brothers. This is a meaningful insight as we look at this second epistle of John.

In his later years, John remained in Jerusalem among the leadership there, although he was not present during Paul's last visit. His subsequent history, however, is unrecorded. He appears to have retired at Ephesus, but at what time we're not quite sure. John's three epistles were probably written from Ephesus, but that's a conjecture too. He suffered persecution, was banished to Patmos where he wrote the book of Revelation. And then he returned again to Ephesus, where he finally died around A.D. 98.

BACKGROUND: EPHESUS

Ephesus was the capital of proconsular Asia, which was the western part of Asia Minor. It was colonized principally from Athens; in the time of the Romans it bore the title of "the first and greatest metropolis of Asia." It was distinguished by the Temple of Diana, whose chief shrine was there; and for its open-air theater, which was the largest in the world, capable of containing 50,000 spectators. Many Jews took up their residence in this city, and here the seeds of the Gospel were sown immediately after Pentecost (Acts 2:9; 6:9).

PAUL'S MINISTRY AT EPHESUS

Paul first visited Ephesus at the close of his second missionary journey (about A.D. 51) when he was returning from Greece to Syria (Acts 18:18-21). He remained, however, for only a short time, as he was hastening to keep the feast, probably of Pentecost, at Jerusalem; but he left Aquila and Priscilla behind him to carry on the work of spreading the Gospel. During his third missionary journey Paul reached Ephesus from the inland parts of Asia Minor, and tarried there for about three years (Acts 19:1). So successful and abundant were his labors that "all they which dwelt in Asia heard the word of the Lord Jesus, both Jews and Greeks" (Acts 19:10).

On his return from his journey, Paul touched at Miletus, some 30 miles south of Ephesus (Acts 20:15). Sending for the presbyters of Ephesus to meet him there, he delivered to them that touching farewell charge, which is recorded, and in which he warned them in Acts 20:29-31:

> [29]*I know that when I'm gone, savage wolves will come among you and not spare the flock.* [30]*Indeed, some of your own men will arise and distort the truth in order to lure the disciples into following them.* [31]*So be alert! Remember that for three years, night and day, I never stopped tearfully warning each of you.*

Indeed, there was a rise of false teachers (the "Gnostics") that emerged subsequently. This is the very situation that John is dealing with in his letters.

GNOSTICISM

The Gnostics (so-called from the Greek word *gnosis*, which means *knowledge*) are mentioned in John's letters. These heresies promised people "spiritual perfection" if they entered into the teachings and ceremonies prescribed. This "depth" and "full knowledge" could only be enjoyed by those initiated, etc. These were all based on man-made traditions and philosophy, not on divine Truth (see Colossians 2:8).

The Gnostics came to the false conclusion that matter was evil; that a powerful spirit world used material things to attack mankind. They held to a form of astrology, believing that angelic beings associated with heavenly bodies influenced affairs on earth (Colossians 1:16; 2:10, 15). Added to these Eastern speculations was a form of Jewish legalism: the idea that the rite of circumcision was helpful in spiritual development (Colossians 2:11); and the Old Testament dietary laws were also helpful in attaining spiritual perfection (Colossians 2:14-17). Good and evil were derived from rules and regulations (Colossians 2:21).

DOCETIC GNOSTICS

The Docetics (from *dokeo*, "to seem") Gnostics held that Jesus did not have a real human body, but only a phantom body. He was, in fact, an *aeon* and had no real humanity. These views were increasingly prevalent in Ephesus (and elsewhere) and form the challenges that John was dealing within 1 John.

CERINTHIAN GNOSTICS

The Cerinthian Gnostics (followers of the heretic Cerinthus) admitted the humanity of the man Jesus, but claimed that the Messiah was an aeon that came on Jesus at his baptism in the form of a dove and left him on the Cross so that only the man Jesus died.

Some thought that Jesus was "just a man"—similar to Christian Science and other phases of "New Thought." Paul deals with this heresy directly. Others held that Jesus was only spiritual, not material; John also deals with these in his three epistles.

This heresy sharpened the issue concerning the Person of the Messiah already set forth in Philippians 2:5-11. Paul met the issue squarely and powerfully portrayed his full-length portrait of Jesus the Messiah as the Son of God and the Son of Man (both deity and humanity) in opposition to both types of Gnostics. So then Colossians seems written expressly for our own day when so many are trying to rob Jesus the Messiah of his deity.

These errors are important to understand since these attacks on the deity of the Messiah are just as prevalent today as then. Each cult group involves a strategy to misrepresent some aspect of revealed truth in regards to the Messiah and His redemptive work.

These views undermined the very foundations of the Christian faith, and attacked the person and work of Jesus the Messiah. To them, He was but one of God's many "emanations" and not the very Son of God, come in the flesh. The Incarnation means "God *with us*" (Matthew 1:23), but these false teachers claimed that God was keeping His distance from us! When we trust the Son of God, there is no need for any intermediary beings between us and heaven![1]

THE AGE OF SYNCRETISM

These false teachings were a combination of many things: Jewish legalism, Oriental philosophies, pagan astrology, mysticism, asceticism, with a touch of Christianity. Here was "something for everybody"—an attempt to harmonize and unite many different schools of thought into a composite religion. These teachers claimed that they were *not* denying the Christian faith, but only lifting it to a "higher level." Do we have any of these heresies today? Indeed, and they are ever more dangerous!

NOTHING "NEW" IN THE "NEW AGE"!

Every modern erroneous cult is some ancient Satanic heresy revived. Every "new" heresy has been anticipated by the Holy Spirit. Satan has nothing new to offer. We live in a day when religious toleration is interpreted to mean "one religion is as good as another." Many people try to take the best from various religions and fabricate their own. To them the Messiah is only one of several

---

1   For further reading, see http://www.bibletools.org/index.cfm/fuseaction/Bible.show/sVerseID/29475/eVerseID/29477/opt/BN/RTD/RBN.

great religious teachers, with no more authority than they have. He may be prominent, but certainly not *preeminent.*

When we make Jesus the Messiah and the Bible only a *part* of a total religious system or philosophy, we cease to give Him preeminence. When we strive for "spiritual perfection" or "fullness" by means of formulas, disciplines, or rituals, we go backward rather than forward. We must beware of mixing our Christian faith with such alluring things as yoga, transcendental meditation, Oriental mysticism, and the like. We must also beware of the "deeper life" teachers who offer a system for victory and fullness that bypasses devotion to Jesus the Messiah. In all things, He must have preeminence!

THE MESSAGE OF 2 JOHN

The message of John's second epistle is essential for a proper perspective of what he said in his first epistle. It is rather remarkable how timely these letters are for *today*: The cultural war being waged in our country has deep spiritual significance—far beyond simply cultural or political philosophies. Both 2 John and 3 John are short, individual, personal letters. We don't know the order that the three were written; many assume they were written after John's exile at Patmos. It would seem that 2 John was written to the same community as 1 John, but at an earlier date (since the false teachers evidently still had access to the church in 2 John, but had separated from it in 1 John (1 John 2:19).

Furthermore, by the time of Patmos, Ephesus was diligent in doctrine, but had "lost their first love" (Revelation 2:1-7). False teachers not only invaded the churches, they also tried to influence Christian homes. It is significant that the pagan left continually embarks on a militant campaign against the family. As goes the home, so goes the Church and the nation. The family is an important target in Satan's war against truth. Second John may also be the most neglected book of the New Testament. (And if one of my suspicions proves correct, it may also harbor one of the biggest surprises!)

THE TEXT OF 2 JOHN

¹From: The Elder
To: The chosen lady and her children, whom I genuinely
love, and not only I but also all who know the truth,
²that is present in us and will be with us forever.
³Grace, mercy, and peace will be with us from God the
Father and from Jesus the Messiah, the Father's Son,
in truth and love.
⁴I was overjoyed to find some of your children living
truthfully, just as the Father has commanded us. ⁵Dear lady,
I am now requesting of you that we all continue to love
one another. It is not as though I am writing to give you
a new commandment, but one that we have had from the
beginning. ⁶And this is what demonstrates love: that we live
according to God's commandments. Just as you have heard
from the beginning what he commanded, you must live by it.
⁷For many deceivers have gone out into the world. They refuse
to acknowledge Jesus the Messiah as having become human.
Any such person is a deceiver and an antichrist. ⁸See to it
that you don't destroy what we have worked for, but that you
receive your full reward. ⁹Everyone who does not remain true
to the teaching of the Messiah, but goes beyond it, does not
have God. The person who remains true to the teaching of the
Messiah has both the Father and the Son. ¹⁰If anyone comes
to you but does not present his teachings, do not receive him
into your house or even welcome him, ¹¹because the one who
welcomes him shares in his evil deeds.
¹²Although I have a great deal to write to you, I would
prefer not to use paper and ink. Instead, I hope to come
to you and talk face to face, so that our joy may be complete.
¹³The children of your chosen sister greet you.

Who is the "Elect Lady"?

Who is "the elect lady"? This identity is the primary mystery of the letter. The view that the term should be taken as a symbolic description of the Christian Church has occurred consistently since as early as Jerome [Jerome (*Ep. Xi. Ad Ageruchiam*). Later Calovius, Whiston, Michaelis, Augusti, Hofmann (Weissagung u. Erfüllung, II. P.321, and Schriftbew., I. P.226ff); Hilgenfeld (1855), Ewald, Candlish, Barnes, Huther, and, more recently, Harris, Marshall, Plummer, Stedman, Vines, McGee, Wiersbe, Walvoord] and other modern commentators.

The view of believers as "children of the Church" may have been comfortable for Jerome, et al., for ecclesiastical reasons, but it flies in the face of Scriptural usage. We are "children of God," not "children of the Church." The Church is presented as a virgin (2 Corinthians 11:2) and the bride (Jn 3:29; Rev 18:23; 21:2, 9; 22:17; cf. Eph 5:22-27) It is also significant that this word does not appear elsewhere in this signification. The further allusion to the sister (v.13) would seem fatal to this view, but for the preponderance of expositional history.

The Alternative Assumption: The Mother of Jesus the Messiah

This seems clear from a straight-forward reading. The writer knows her sister and her sister's children (v.13). *This view would make this the only book in the Bible specifically addressed to a woman.* John uses a plural (vv. 6, 8, 10, 12) and an individual (vv. 1, 4, 5, 13). The fact that he embraces others as well in passing doesn't alter the intended addressee. The family of the "Elect Lady" is clearly in view.

A Provocative Conjecture

Who would be the *most* "Elect Lady" in the entire Bible? To me, the most likely *prima facie* suggestion is that the recipient of this intimate letter is the most "elect" of all women, the very one that Jesus Himself entrusted to John's personal care: Mary, the mother of Jesus (John 19:26, 27) and she did have a sister (v. 13; John 19:25).

This view, however, is not even discussed among modern commentators.[2] Most Biblical believers, from their revulsion to the tragic and heretical deification of Mary by the Roman Catholic Church, tend to dismiss her and ignore her situation and predicament. (We cannot miss the dismissive allusion at her prompting during the wedding at Cana in John 2:4.)

We know so little of her subsequent history from the Scriptures: there are minimal allusions in the Book of Acts (1:14). She apparently remained in the care of John in his retirement in Ephesus. (This conjecture would indicate that 2 John would have been written earlier than A.D. 90, since Mary would have been about a century old by then.) At any rate, most of what is commonly published by the Roman Catholic Church has been contrived by subsequent Popes to promote their doctrinal heresies, etc.

The "Elect Lady" is loved "*by all who love the truth.*" Who else could this fit? This, too, seems to point to far more than simply a prominent personage within the local church! If this suspicion is correct, it places an entirely unique complexion on the letter, and also provides a number of significant insights.

> [1]*From: The Elder*
> *To: The chosen lady and her children, whom I genuinely love, and not only I but also all who know the truth,* [2]*that is present in us and will be with us forever.*

The phrase "...and her children..." should make the case unequivocal: Mary's sister was also at the cross when John was called to take Mary under his provision (John 19:25-27). Most expositions of this letter highlight the prominence of "truth," in concert with "love" as the keynote of the letter. John uses the word "truth" five times in the first four verses. He uses the word "love" four times. If you take love away from truth, you don't have Christian love. Real love always operates within the sphere of truth.

---

2   Except see Knauer: Stud. U. Krit., 1833, Part 2, p.452ff; q.v. Huther, J. E., *Critical and Exegetical Handbook to the General Epistles of James, Peter, John, and Jude* (translated from the German) (11 vols.), Funk and Wagnalls, 1884.

WHAT IS TRUTH?

As Pilate's cynical question still echoes, Jesus' declaration is conclusive and comprehensive: "I am the Way, the Truth, and the Life" (John 14:6). Here "the Truth" suggests a personal appellation: The Truth "is present in us" and "shall be with us forever." John is using it as a title of Jesus the Messiah, just as he so often uses the *Logos*, the Word (John 1:1-3, 14; 1 John 5:7; Revelation 19:13).

It is astonishing to observe our institutions now denying the very existence of that which they were founded to discover. As if 2 + 2 = 4 is subjective and subject to debate! In any case, Truth is unchangeable. "What is true is not new; and what is new is not true."

> *³Grace, mercy, and peace will be with us from God the Father and from Jesus the Messiah, the Father's Son, in truth and love.*

Grace? Mercy? Love? Could you write a short reflective paper on the distinctives *between* them? Ephesians 2:4-5 combines all three:

> *⁴But God, who is rich in mercy, because of his great love for us ⁵even when we were dead because of our offenses, made us alive together with the Messiah (by grace you have been saved),...*

Grace is getting what we don't deserve; Mercy is not getting what we do. As Lewis Sperry Chafer explains:

> *Love is that in God which existed before He would care to exercise mercy or grace.*

J. Vernon McGee said:

> *It is interesting that love never saved a sinner. The love of God caused God to move in the direction of mercy and grace; it caused Him to exercise mercy and grace.*

The Apostle Paul summarizes the working of grace and righteousness together in Romans 3:26:

*He wanted to demonstrate at the present time that he
himself is righteous and that he justifies anyone who has the
faithfulness of Jesus.*

Salvation is not only an expression of the love of God; it is also an expression of the justice and righteousness of God. As Hal Lindsey summarizes things, the word "GRACE" may be thought of as an acronym that spells out the phrase:

"God's Riches At Christ's Expense."

It has been suggested that John's emphasis of Jesus' paternity—"Son of the Father"—to the recipient links—and equates—the Father with the Son. The paternal emphasis in verse 3 would have had very specific implications for Mary. Can you imagine the burden Mary had to endure throughout her entire adult life from the cloud of the ostensible illegitimacy that was imputed to her first pregnancy? (Cf. The aspersions cast in John 8:41. Jesus *then* discusses *their* parentage in 8:44! Also compare the childhood insights of Psalm 69:7-12.) Now with respect to the sonship of Jesus, 1 John 2:23 tells us:

*[23]No one who denies the Son has the Father. The person who
acknowledges the Son also has the Father.*

In John 10:30, Jesus is quoted as saying, "I and the Father are one." And in John 8:58, ""Truly, I tell all of you emphatically, before there was an Abraham, I AM!"

In each of these instances, the leadership understood what He was claiming: they tried to stone Him for blasphemy. Furthermore, this was the specific indictment for which they crucified Him (Matthew 26:63-66).

*[63]... Then the high priest told him, "I command you by the
living God to tell us if you are the Messiah, the Son of God!"
[64]Jesus told him, "You have said so. Nevertheless I tell you,
from now on you will see 'the Son of Man seated at the right
hand of Power' and 'coming on the clouds of heaven.'"*

⁶⁵Then the high priest tore his robes and said, "He has blasphemed! Why do we still need witnesses? Listen! You yourselves have just heard the blasphemy! ⁶⁶What is your verdict?"
They replied, "He deserves to die!"

It is astonishing that so many are unaware of the numerous claims of Jesus' Godship! (Even the august pseudo-scholars of the Jesus Seminar seem willing to ignore who they are really dealing with! Perhaps, if they cast enough votes they hope He'll resign!)

⁴I was overjoyed to find some of your children living truthfully, just as the Father has commanded us.

By using the phrase "some of your children," John appears to be reminding us that Jesus was raised in a family of at least seven other siblings: five sons and two sisters (Matthew 13:55-56; Mark 5:3). James and Jude became believers after the resurrection; in fact, they each wrote books in the New Testament that bear their names. Jesus is recorded by the Apostle Paul as having appeared to James after his resurrection (cf. 1 Corinthians 15:7).

The Greek text of this verse actually indicates "some" of her children rather than all of them (cf. John 7:5). If our surmise is correct—and it is only a surmise—some of the others may also have become believers in later years after his resurrection.

By using the phrase "living truthfully," the issue here, as in all of John's three letters, is that love and truth must be practiced, for this is the meaning of the verb "living." "To life truthfully" means to obey it. It is easier to study the truth, or even argue about the truth, than it is to obey it. Knowing the truth is more than giving assent to a series of doctrines; it means that the believer's life is controlled by a love for the truth and a desire to magnify the truth.

⁵Dear lady, I am now requesting of you that we all continue to love one another. It is not as though I am writing to give you a new commandment, but one that we have had from the beginning.

We suggest that by using the term "from the beginning," the recipient was not a latecomer: she was there "from the beginning" (cf. vv. 5 & 6). The "we" carries a provocative joint identity. In the exhortation to "love one another," we are reminded that to love is a commandment. John's exhortation here is a reminder of what Jesus had said in John 14:15 during the time of his mortality: "If you love me, keep my commandments." Real love is a choice, not an emotion. I choose to love you. When I obey, I do what God tells me to do.[3]

>*⁶And this is what demonstrates love: that we live according to God's commandments. Just as you have heard from the beginning what he commanded, you must live by it.*

We should not presume that any of us are beyond the need for exhortation or encouragement. Why would Mary—a very blessed but very human believer—be any exception? Mary was subject to the same frailties as all of us: pride and doubts, and thus also needed frequent encouragement, counsel, and, perhaps, exhortation.

A tendency toward pride would certainly be her serious challenge: the most blessed of all women who had ever walked the earth! Think about it. What would be her "thorn in the flesh"? (cf. 2 Corinthians 12:7-9). Both truth and love can be perverted. In view of the onslaught of the Gnostic heresies and doubts may well have brought unique challenges for Mary, especially!

KEEPING MARY IN PERSPECTIVE

The Apostle John reminds Mary in 2 John 7:

>*⁷For many deceivers have gone out into the world. They refuse to acknowledge Jesus the Messiah as having become human. Any such person is a deceiver and an antichrist.*

Here is a clear response to the prevalent Gnostic teachings. They were teaching that Jesus the Messiah was not really a person; just a phantom. When He walked He didn't leave a footprint!

By claiming that Jesus the Messiah still exists in his post-resurrection state "as having become human," we invite the reader

---

3   For further reading, we commend to your reading Nancy Missler's work , *The Way of Agape*.

to note John's surprising use of the present (i.e., continuous) tense nuance in this verse: for John, Jesus the Messiah had come and still exists "as a human being." In the first chapter of John's Gospel, he emphasizes,

> *¹⁴The Word became flesh and lived among us. We gazed on his glory, the kind of glory that belongs to the Father's uniquely existing Son, who is full of grace and truth.*

In his sermon that we call 1 John, the Apostle opens his letter with a similar emphasis:

> *¹What existed from the beginning, what we have heard, what we have seen with our eyes, what we observed and touched with our own hands—this is the Word of life!*

THE ENEMIES OF THE MESSIAH

The Pharisees were the conservatives of Jesus' day; the Sadducees were the liberals. Both were in trouble. However, the Sadducees were the greatest enemies that the Messiah had and were the main instigators of the first persecution of the Church.

The Pharisees with the Sadducees were the leaders of the persecution of the Lord Jesus. But after the death of the Lord, most of the Pharisees dropped the whole affair. They lost interest in persecuting him or his followers; in fact, many of them became Christians (Acts 3 & 4).

A Pharisee named Nicodemus was converted, as were many priests (cf. Acts 6:7). There is no account in Scripture of a Sadducee ever coming to the Messiah for salvation. *The acid test of the Sadducees was the resurrection, as it is today among the "liberals."*

The prevalent Gnostic teachings would have presented a disconcerting problem for Mary. (Why would she have been immune to doubts and misgivings?)

The literal Greek grammar of verse 7 mentions "the antichrist"—the Greek has the definite article. The prefix "anti-" actually means "instead of," even though the modern use is sometimes mistakenly interpreted as emphasizing the concept of being "against." Both are, of course, true.[4]

> [8]*See to it that you don't destroy what we have worked for,*
> *but that you receive your full reward.*

It may be disturbing for some Christians to learn that it's possible to lose their reward (literally, "wages" in the Greek text). This was true even of Mary! Otherwise, John would not have written this verse to her!

None of us should take anything for granted. We cannot lose that which Jesus completed; but we can fail to retain that which "*we* have worked for," those things which derive from our own faithfulness. Every believer ought to be working for a reward, and be able to hear Him say, as recorded in Matthew 25:21:[5]

> ... *"Well done, good and trustworthy servant! Since you've*
> *been trustworthy with a small amount, I'll put you in charge*
> *of a large amount. Come and share your master's joy!"*

On the Exclusivity of the Gospel

> [9]*Everyone who does not remain true to the teaching of the*
> *Messiah, but goes beyond it, does not have God. The person*
> *who remains true to the teaching of the Messiah has both the*
> *Father and the Son.*

John was not one to suggest that all religious teachings are true in one way or another, and that we should not be critical just as long as people are sincere. To John, there was a deadly difference. He that does not have the Messiah does not have God.

John warns against going beyond the limits, which means to go past as to turn aside; thus, to extend beyond the pale of orthodoxy. This is the characteristic of every cult. They always have some new information or insight that goes beyond the clear and express

---

4   John does not use this term "antichrist" in the Book of Revelation.
5   For a fuller treatment of this subject, see Missler, Chuck and Nancy Missler. *The Kingdom, Power & Glory,* published by Koinonia House.

doctrines of God. Every cult finds a new way to deny the deity of Jesus the Messiah.

By referring to "remaining" true, we should bear in mind that even Mary, of all people, may have had particular difficulties in this area. In any case, she certainly would have been drawn into the raging controversies over the real nature of Jesus. Incidentally, the verb "remain" is intended to be a permanent arrangement.

> *[10]If anyone comes to you but does not present his teachings,*
> *do not receive him into your house or even welcome him,*
> *[11]because the one who welcomes him shares in his evil deeds.*

Let us also remember that hospitality—especially in those rough times—was extremely critical to the ministry. The "hospitality industry" of motels and related services came later. The inns of those early days were neither safe nor adequate. Traveling pastors or teachers needed homes to stay in (cf. 3 John 5-8).

HOSPITALITY

Paul stayed in the home of Aquila and Priscilla when he was in Corinth. The situation is quite different today. In fact, most traveling speakers prefer the privacy of commercial accommodations for study and prayer, which is rarely equivalent when one is being received in a private residence, however well intended.

Christians are admonished to open their homes to visitors (Romans 12:13; 1 Timothy 3:2; 5:3-10; Hebrews 13:2; 1 Peter 4:8-10). But the context here can be considered providing respite to itinerant speakers: John is saying that believers must not let the poison of false doctrine get into our home.

There is a colorful legend concerning John's attitude toward a notable heretic in Ephesus: a cultist and false teacher by the name of Cerinthus, who taught that Jesus was the natural son of Joseph and Mary, not God come in the flesh. One day at the local bath house, when Cerinthus arrived, John jumped out of the water, got his clothes and towels, and took off running, and exclaimed, "Let us hurry from this house, lest it fall on us. Cerinthus, the enemy of truth, is here."

FALSE TEACHERS

John did not want any of God's children to give a false teacher the impression that his heretical doctrine was acceptable, become infected because of association and possible friendship, and give the false teacher ammunition to use at the next place he stopped. John is certainly admonishing us to not receive or encourage false teachers representing anti-Christian groups. This is another grave reason that you should investigate everything you give to as a Christian, because if you are giving to the wrong thing, God considers you a partner in it.

> *12Although I have a great deal to write to you, I would prefer not to use paper and ink. Instead, I hope to come to you and talk face to face, so that our joy may be complete. 13The children of your chosen sister greet you.*

This verse also argues for the addressee to be a specific individual. Since John's Gospel mentions that Mary did have at least one sister (John 19:25), John's mention of the children of the recipient's sister may assist us in clinching our theory that the recipient of this letter was Mary, the mother of Jesus.

THE MARIAN APPARITIONS

The deification of Mary by the Roman Catholic Church represents far more than simply a heterodox departure from the Biblical faith. In addition to be a blasphemy on the deity, role, and person of Jesus the Messiah, this pagan contrivance appears to be the continuing vehicle for the execution of strategic demonic activities of the most sinister sort.

Most Protestant observers tend to dismiss the sequence of sightings and encounters with what purports to be the Virgin Mary as simply hallucinations, hoaxes, or incidents of well-intentioned religious hysteria. While some of these incidents may well be, there are a significant number of them that evidence clear supernatural involvements and deserve our serious caution! For instance, the Visions at Fatima, Portugal on 13 May 1917 and on 13 October by three children. It has been reported that there were ostensibly 70,000 witnesses to the apparitions.

BIBLIOGRAPHY

Barnes, Albert, *Notes on the New Testament, James to Jude*, Barnes Notes (14 vols.), Baker Book House, Grand Rapids, MI (reprinted from 1884 edition by Blackie & Son, London).

Huther, J. E., *Critical and Exegetical Handbook to the General Epistles of James, Peter, John, and Jude* (translated from the German) (11 vols.), Funk and Wagnalls, 1884.

Knauer: Stud. U. Krit., 1833, Part 2, p.452ff; q.v. Huther, J. E., *Critical and Exegetical Handbook to the General Epistles of James, Peter, John, and Jude* (translated from the German) (11 vols.), Funk and Wagnalls, 1884.

Marshall, I. Howard, *The Epistles of John*, William B. Eerdmans Publishing Company, Grand Rapids, MI 1978.

McGee, J. Vernon, *Through the Bible* (5 vols), Thomas Nelson, Nashville, TN 1983.

Plummer, A., C. Cemeance, et al., *The Epistles of St. John*, The Pulpit Commentary, William B. Eermans Publishing Company, Grand Rapids, MI 1950.

Stedman, Ray C., *Expository Studies in 1 John*, Word Books, Waco, TX 1980. Vines, Jerry, Exploring 1-2-3 John, Loizeaux Brothers, Neptune, NJ 1989.

Walvoord, John F., and Zuck, Roy B., ed., *The Bible Knowledge Commentary*, Chariot Victor Publishing, Cook Communications, Colorado Springs, CO 1983.

Wiersbe, Warren W. , *The Bible Exposition Commentary* (2 Vols), Scripture Press, Wheaton, IL 1989.

AN INTRODUCTION
TO THE
KOINONIA INSTITUTE

BY *CHARLES W. MISSLER, PHD*
CHAIRMAN AND FOUNDER
KOINONIA INSTITUTE

You are invited to undertake a lifelong adventure, exploring the Word of God among an international fellowship without borders — neither intellectual nor geographic. This is an opportunity to "bloom where you are planted" by studying the Bible — and related topics — in virtual classrooms on the Internet, while discovering the unique calling on your own life and preparing for the challenges which will inevitably emerge on your personal horizon.

This is not for everyone. It is designed for those who are truly committed to becoming an Ambassador for the Coming King. Here you will find flexible paths of achievement without any straightjackets of presumption or tradition. We are non-denominational, but decidedly from a conservative, traditional, evangelical perspective.

We believe that the world is heading into extremely turbulent times that will test all of our presumptions and beliefs. It is our objective to identify, encourage, and equip leadership for the challenges ahead.

Koinonia Institute is not just about academic achievement. Your membership gives you access to numerous other materials and resources, including weekly downloadable studies, weekly intelligence updates, discussion forums, audio and video interviews from around the world, and privileged surveillance of the strategic

229

trends monitored by the Institute; proprietary archives of relevant research; private forums with nationally known personalities; and, other involvements with distinguished members of the Fellowship.

After reviewing the emerging programs, pray seriously about joining us and assisting us in developing this unique Fellowship.

MISSION STATEMENT

Koinonia Institute is dedicated to training and equipping the serious Christian to sojourn in today's world.

For several decades the ministry of Koinonia House has been to create, develop, and distribute educational materials for those who take the Bible seriously as the inerrant Word of God. As an affiliated ministry, the Koinonia Institute is focused on three supporting areas:

- To provide instructional programs to facilitate serious study of the Bible among thinking Christians;

- To encourage and facilitate both individual and small group weekly study programs for personal growth; and

- To research, monitor and publish information to stimulate awareness of the strategic trends which impact our times and our personal ministries and stewardships.

The Institute is committed to accomplishing these goals through a program of lifelong learning, utilizing Internet resources as a means to do this and creating and developing an intelligence network among its members. Koinonia Institute is formed around three tracks — The Berean, The Issachar, and The Koinonos, which can lead to a two and four year degree in Biblical Studies. For information about each track, please see the Student Handbook.

Visit our web site at https://koinoniainstitute.org.

INDEX OF
SUBJECTS AND SCRIPTURES

ABOUT THE AUTHOR

WILLIAM P. WELTY, PH.D.

Dr. Welty (http://williamwelty.com) is the Executive Director of the ISV Foundation of Bellflower, California, producers of the *Holy Bible: International Standard Version.* He is a graduate (M.Div., 1978) of Trinity Evangelical Divinity School of Deerfield, Illinois and holds a Ph.D. degree in Christian Communications (2005) from Louisiana Baptist University. Dr. Welty is a member of the Board of Directors of *Koinonia House* and serves as Scholar in Residence on the faculty of the Koinonia Institute in Reporoa, New Zealand.

ABOUT THE HOLY BIBLE: INTERNATIONAL STANDARD VERSION

The *International Standard Version* is produced by the ISV Foundation of Bellflower, California directly from the Hebrew and Aramaic texts of the Hebrew Scriptures and from the Greek New Testament, using a team of conservative Biblical and lay scholars drawn from the international Christian community. It is published in a variety of electronic formats, including Amazon Kindle® and Barnes and Noble Nook® editions, as well as Adobe Acrobat® PDF formats and in HTML format for use by webmasters. Visit http://isv.org to learn more.

ALSO BY THE AUTHOR:

A Person of Substance: Word Studies on the Character Qualities of Christian Leadership. (Bellflower, CA: ISV Foundation, 2014)

A User's Manual for the Bible: A Simple and Practical Answer to the Challenge Faced by the Church from the Emergent Church Heresy. (Bellflower, CA: ISV Foundation, 2014)

Anselm Writes Again: A 2st Century Scholar Revisits a Christian Classic. (Bellflower, CA: ISV Foundation, 2015)

I, Jesus: an Autobiography. (Reporoa, New Zealand: Koinonia Institute, 2014)

I, Jesus: the Messiah's Manifesto: Studies in the Sermon on the Mount. (Bellflower, CA: ISV Foundation, 2015)

I, Jesus: the World's Last Emperor: Jesus of Nazareth Speaks about the End of the World and How he will Make it Happen. (Bellflower, CA: ISV Foundation, 2015)

On Reaffirming the Marriage Covenant. (Bellflower, CA: ISV Foundation, 2015)

On the Validity of the State of Israel. (Reporoa, New Zealand: Koinonia Institute, 2015)

Since He Wrote about Me: Jesus of Nazareth speaks in his own words about the authenticity, reliability, and accuracy of the Hebrew Scriptures. (Bellflower, CA: ISV Foundation, 2016)

Surviving God's Discipline of a Nation. (Bellflower, CA: ISV Foundation, 2015)

Ten Test Questions for the World's Finest Woman: A Protestant Theologian Looks at the life of Mary, the Mother of Jesus of Nazareth. (Coeur d'Alene, ID: Koinonia House, 2016)

As Contributing Author and/or Editor

A Harmony of the Gospels from the International Standard Version. Edited by William Welty. (Toluca Lake, CA: Davidson Press, 2013)

Between Christ and Muhammad: The Irreconcilable Differences of Christianity and Islam. (Yorba Linda, CA: Davidson Press, 2002)

Encyclopedia of Bible Difficulties. By Dr. Gleason L. Archer. Contributing researcher: William Welty. (Zondervan Publishing, 1982)

Golgotha: The Search for the True Location of Christ's Crucifixion. By Dr. Robert Cornuke. Contributing editor: William Welty. (Coeur d'Alene, ID: Koinonia House: 2016)

Holy Bible: International Standard Version. Associate Editor: William Welty. (Bellflower, CA: ISV Foundation 1996-2016)

How to Be a People Helper. By Dr. Gary R. Collins. Contributing researcher: William Welty. (Vision House: 1976)

Ministry, Finance, and Ethics. (Irvine, CA: Fieldstead Institute, 1984)

Secret History: An Eyewitness Account of the Rise of Mormonism. Translated from John Ahmanson's original Danish edition by Dr. Gleason L. Archer; edited by William Welty. (Chicago: Moody Press, 1984)

See http://williamwelty.com to learn more.